I0099271

CONCRETE
Situations

Vol. 1

By Crystal Darks

Concrete Situations

Copyright © 2015 by Crystal Darks

All rights reserved. No part of this publication may be reproduced, distributed, or transmitted in any form or by any means, including photocopying, recording, or other electronic or mechanical methods, without the prior written permission of the publisher, except in the case of brief quotations embodied in critical reviews and certain other noncommercial uses permitted by copyright law. For permission requests, write to the publisher, addressed "Attention: Permissions Coordinator," @ authorc.darks82@yahoo.com

ISBN 978-0578158716

Summary: Young, beautiful Paris has the lifestyle most women would kill for – she's rich, beautiful and married to a very powerful man. But things aren't as happy as they seem from the outside looking in. And when her husband – a well-known drug lord – is busted for his crimes and sent to prison, Paris is left alone to raise their children by herself. Soon, the skeletons of her husband's misdeeds come out of the closet, and she becomes entangled in not only his – but his whole family's – dark and strange history. Will she keep it together, or will she hit a brick wall in these Concrete Situations?

Concrete Situations: *Vol. 1*

ACKOWLEDGEMENTS

First, I would like to thank God for blessing me with this beautiful gift to write. Without him, none of this would be possible. And to my Grandmother, Thelma Darks, who is my sweet angel. I thank you for everything you have done. The same morals and values you instilled in me are the same ones that I plan to instill in my baby girl, Faith. Words can't explain how much I miss you, and I love you so much.

I'd also like to acknowledge my sweet angel Grandmother, Barbara Turner. I miss your warmth, your smile, and your love. Grandpa Eugene Darks, I know that I never got the chance to meet you, but I will see you on the other side and we can catch up. I love you. To my Uncle Geno and Uncle Darryl, I love and miss you both so much. Uncle Geno, thank you for being that father figure in my life.

To my Cousin Seneca Darks - even though I don't remember much of you, we will always be connected. Due to the fact I was born on your first birthday, I carry a part of you with me, and cherish it as I remain close to your father, Jackie Ray McClellan, your grandmother, Billie McClellan, and your siblings, Eric, Nicole, Destini, and Justice. Every year on our birthday we all connect. That's my way of celebrating with you, until we meet again on the other side. I love you.

I'd like to also acknowledge my Aunt, Sharon Moss. I still replay your words of wisdom over and over in my head. I miss and love you dearly.

And my baby girl, Faith Sherrell Lockhart. Always remember that a fountain of love will always pour from my heart to you. The day you were born, I started to look at life differently. You are the reason why I do all that I do. When

I look at you, you give me the drive and motivation to continue to better myself every day. Without you there is no me. Mommy loves you so much!

To my Mother, Felicia Darks. I thank you for bringing me into this world. I'm deeply grateful for everything that you do, and know that the depth of love that I have for you is boundless.

To my second mother, Lori McDonald, thank you for your open arms. Thank you for loving me as if I was one of your biological children.

And to my siblings, Andre Collins and Cory Collins, I love the two of you so much. You both bring such a warm smile to my heart when we are in each other's presence. I thank God for blessing me with you in my life, and I wouldn't have it any other way. And to my Aunt, Brenda Turner – you already know you're my Ace. I love you.

My Uncle Donnell, thank you for always being in my corner and having my back. I love you. And Aunt Polly, thank you for everything that you've done. I will always remember when you took me in to live with you, even when you already had three other kids of your own. I'm blessed to have been surrounded by so many compassionate and kind souls in my life.

April Patton, I'm not sure where you are at this moment, but if you are reading this, please know that I appreciate everything that you've done for me, and I love you. Yvonne Brown, thank you for being a mother figure in my life. I will never forget you, and I love you. Toni Mendez, and my Cousin Regaishala Ward thank you for providing a safe place for me. I love you. My big Cousin Archie Thomas and Mandy Sterling thanks for always being there, and taking me in when I needed you, I love you.

My cousin, Starr Sykes, I thank you for being in my corner, and for not judging me. You have seen all of my craziness, and I'm surprised that you haven't disowned me yet! I love you so very, very much. To all of my families –

Darks, Collins, Clemons, McDonald, Sykes, and Wilson – I love you all so much. And, of course, my dear friends and sisters – Erikka Williams, Tealithia Pittman, Teffanie Price, Stephanie Cuellar, Treyon Harris, Shaqu'atta Benson, Loretta Davis Guilford, Nicole Lucas, Brandy Russ, Jennifer Southall, Catherine Phiffer, Tasha Bell, Christina Vaughn, Monique Hancock, Denice Hysaw, Kendra McCullough, Camilla Fagan, and Demetrist LaShawn Wallace – thank you all for being good friends, and for being deeply supportive of my every move. My heart wells with love and appreciation for you all.

SPECIAL THANKS

I'd like to give a special thanks to my wonderful editor, Demetrist LaShawn Wallace, CEO of Mind, Body, & Soul Editing Company.

A special thanks also goes out to:
Trina Cleveland, author of *The Pink Elephant in the Middle of The Getto*
Caleb Devine, author of *Bona Fide Hustler.*
A. Adams Jones, author of *Blind Innocence.*
Jessica Wren, author of *The Worst THOTS Ever.*
Tanisha, author of *2^{Nd} Sunday Playing For Keeps*
Tranea Prosser, author of *Celibacy: What Was I Thinking?*
Tawanna Jackson - CEO of She Smiles Entertainment
Sonny BX, author of *With Friendz Like Theze*
Bigg Mike, author of *R.O.C. Hard*
Rose Chase Smith, author of *She Got Game* and *Nothing Like Me*

I want to thank you all for being a phone call away. Thank you for that push that I desperately needed at times. Believe it or not you all kept me going. Much love to you all.

Crystal Darks

Why? Why me? Those were the questions that constantly popped in my head. They were questions that I often asked myself. And I sometimes even found myself screaming those questions from just beneath the surface of a river of tears. As I struggled there, fighting to keep my head above water, something that my mother always told me came to my mind, *"You are not to question God."*

Trust. Is the issue that I have because of all the broken promises, hurt, abandonment, lies, abuse, and a plate full of bull crap that has been served to me on a silver platter throughout my life that I'm sure I never ordered from the menu.

Faith. Was what I had to walk by in this cold world. I managed to stay bundled up and pull through, though, because it was nobody but God who navigated me through my situations.

Sunshine. Is what I found after pulling through the rain, hurricanes, tornadoes, blizzards, and earthquakes in life. After all of that, I sit here with a smile on my face, thanking Him for being with me through my struggles. Without God, I never would have made it.

Prologue

I've been told a thousand times that any woman would give anything to be in my shoes. Hell, if that's the case, I'm ready to hand over these Versace pumps at any given moment and let the next one take a walk down this treacherous road of silent heartache and pain.

See, people only saw one side of my marriage when my husband and I were out in public. They never got to really see what went on behind our closed doors. For three long years, I painted the perfect picture for everyone. I was the perfect wife, donned with the best designer clothes and most luxurious jewelry. My husband bought me the most expensive make-up, which worked wonders when I needed to cover up the bruises he left on my face. Two coats of concealer was all I needed to erase the marks on my skin, but it would take more to erase the marks in my heart. Through all this pain, though, I maintained a smirk.

My husband, Bradley Frost, the biggest wolf in sheep's clothing. He caught me at the tender age of eighteen, greener than spinach, with no clue as to what life was all about. How could I ever know how cold the world was? Well, I guess you can say I was "young and dumb."

He was only five years older than I was, but with the type of father he had growing up, he had already been exposed to a different kind of world than I knew. Warning signs and red flags continued to hit me in my face, but what did my young, dumb self do? I ignored every last one of them.

Just about every person in Austin would be in my ear, saying, "*Girl, you better be careful. Don't you know that him and his father associate with the Lopez family?*" Or I would hear, "*Girl, that man done sold more coke and heroin than McDonald's sold happy meals.*" But I didn't entertain those warnings.

It was easy to ignore them, too, being as lonely and lost as I was. I had recently lost my mother, and right after her funeral, my fourteen year-old sister went to live with her Auntie on her father's side of the family. And just like that, the only two people that I had in my life who ever loved me were gone. So when Bradley came along with his first aid kit, showering me with love, gifts and everything else a young girl in my position ever wanted, I told myself that only a fool would care if he's associating with the Lopez family or not. He was nothing but sweet to me, and in some strange way, he was sort of like the father that I never had; a void was finally filled in my life, and I felt safe and secure. And that feeling is what kept me by his side. But I clearly didn't know of the consequences that I was gonna have to deal with later down the road.

Chapter One

As a waiter walked by with a tray full of bubbling champagne, my arm automatically made an attempt to take one, but then I remembered I was still breast feeding my four month old baby girl, Brielle. I needed something to calm my nerves, though, due the fact I was somewhere that I didn't want to be. We were at my husband's father's 50th birthday party at their mansion out in Westlake Hills. I refused to call him my father-in-law, because the man had never liked me for shit, for whatever reason, and that's exactly how he treated me. Now his wife on the other hand, Mrs. Gloria Frost, was sweet as pie, and she was just as pretty as could be, with her slender catwalk figure and a set of eyes that looked like shiny, brown marbles. In some ways, she reminded me so much of my mother.

Even though I really didn't want to be at this party, I couldn't help but admire the place. Everything was on point, from the decorations to the food that the catering company prepared to the two-tiered chocolate cigar birthday cake that was waiting to be unveiled at just the right moment. Mrs. Frost really bested herself on this one, although I felt like her husband deserved nothing more than a good ol' country ass whoopin, as mean and hateful as he was. I still couldn't figure out, for the life of me, how Mrs. Frost could be married to a mean old bastard like that.

I was tasked with presenting the cake, so when Bradley hit the lights for everyone to gather around the table to sing happy birthday to Mr. Frost, I gently placed it on the table right in front of him. The ugly look he was giving me was visible through the burning candles in the dark; I guess he hated me so much to where he did not want me touching his birthday cake. Ignoring his ignorance, I walked over to my handsome husband, joining in to sing with the rest of the crowd. Bradley wrapped his arms around my waist, kissing me on the cheek. I smiled to myself; now that was the sweet side of my husband that I still loved.

"Ok, now make a wish, Honey," Mrs. Frost said with a grin. But before he could blow out his candles, the lights came on, startling all of the guest.

Then a voice came through the crowd, causing everyone to jump. "I wish you would croak over, you old washed up bastard!" The angry man's voice echoed across the room. Everyone gasped, looking for the culprit for a few confused moments. *"Who the hell is that?"* someone whispered.

Just then, a young man stepped forward with anger burning in his eyes. He couldn't have been more than twenty-five, and I could tell swishas and erb was his best friend by his dark lips, which wore the meanest frown I've ever seen. Mr. Frost looked like he wanted to piss in his pants as his mouth hung wide open. It was funny to see him like this, but I didn't get a chance to enjoy it for long, because Mrs. Frost was already walking over to the guy with her hand covering her mouth, looking like she was about to burst into tears. "Oh my God," she said.

Bradley stood speechlessly, just like his father. They wore identical expressions – scared and maybe a little confused.

Mrs. Frost finally made her way through the crowd, wrapping her arms tight around this unfamiliar guy. Everyone silently watched, confused.

"Oh, God! You sent my baby home," she wailed.

"Yes, Mama. I'm home now," he said quietly in her ear as he held her tight.

I tried to understand what was happening. Bradley never told me he had a brother.

The man looked up at Mr. Frost with madness in his eyes, like he wanted to kill him. Then he directed the angry look toward Bradley.

"Stay put," said Bradley, whispering in my ear. "That's my little brother, Bryce." I nodded as I took a seat, watching what was about to take place. Bradley and his father approached the two of them, standing side by side still in shock.

"Welcome home, bro," Bradley said nervously. "I'm glad you're back."

His brother didn't respond to him, though. Instead, he continued to hold his mother in his arms.

"Son, welcome home," Mrs. Frost said, placing his hand on Bryce's back.

"Don't touch me," Bryce jerked away, making an attempt to swing at Mr. Frost. "Look, old man, I didn't come here for all that; I came to see my mother, and I came to get the money you owe me."

As the guest started to realize what was happening, they began collecting their items from the coat closet and shuffling their way out of the door. My feet were glued to the floor, though, not knowing what to do until my husband spoke.

"Paris, go upstairs and get the kids from the housekeeper," Bradley ordered. I did as I was told.

Ms. Marry, who had worked for the Frost Family for years, was more than willing to help me carry my three year-old baby boy, Bradley Jr down to the car, while I wrapped my four-month old, Brielle, in her soft, pink blanket. The shouting between Bryce, his father and brother woke up the baby as I walked down the stairs and hurried out the door. While Ms. Marry and I put the kids in the car, I could hear Mrs. Frost's cries loud and clear, begging her husband and son's not to fight. I sat in the car, dumbfounded. I still couldn't believe Bradley had a brother and didn't tell me after three years of our marriage.

Moments later, Bradley came storming out the house and to the car. He slammed the door and sped out of the subdivision. Anger was all over him as he drove in silence, I wanted so badly for him to say something, but he didn't. So finally I spoke.

"Why didn't you tell me you had a brother?" He didn't respond at all. Instead, he kept driving, looking straight ahead without a blink in his eye. So I pressed him. "We've been married for three years, and not once have you mentioned that you had a brother. How would you feel if I kept something like that from you? Do you actually think that's right? "

"Paris, shut up and stay out of my family business." he barked. Then he hit his blinker to switch lanes. I hated when he was cold like this; he acted so much like his father. I decided I would leave it alone and ride in silence, but I was feeling so agitated, I popped my lips – something Bradley hated with a passion.

"You pop your lips again, I will see to it that you won't have any lips to pop," he warned.

It made me even more agitated when he talked to me that way. A flash of anger welled up inside of me. Suddenly I grew a pair of balls. I smacked my lips again, acting like he didn't just say anything. "Whatever," I said as I rolled my eyes.

Before I could even finished rolling my eyes, though, his closed fist was saying hello to the left side of my mouth. Blood splattered onto the dash board of the BMW. I quickly clasped the side of my mouth, suppressing a loud cry.

"Now that you have my undivided attention, I'm only going say this one more time – stay *out* of my family business, and stay in *your* lane."

Still holding my mouth, I allowed silent tears to run down my face. I cried quietly, not wanting to wake the kids in the backseat.

I hated when my husband was like this. This had been going on much too long, I thought to myself. Then I noticed a stack of CDs on the floor in front of my feet. I impulsively grabbed the stack and struck him on the right side of his face. He swerved into the other lane as I continued to hit him.

I hoped a cop would pull us over for all the swerving. That would be a way of me getting help, so I could get the kids and just leave. But the more I hit him, the more pissed off he was getting. He blocked my blows as he tried to drive straight on the road, cursing and threatening me all the while. Then he managed to knock all of the CDs out of my hand, and gave me a surprise blow to the side of my face.

"So is that what you want?" he seethed. "Are you satisfied now? You must like getting your ass beat!"

I buried my face into both hands, crying up a storm, hoping and praying that he was finished. My face felt like it was on fire, the whole left side was sore, and my mouth was numb.

"Now, I bet you'll think twice before putting' your hands on me again," he barked, almost waking the kids. After a while, when he was done yelling, I eased my head up and pulled down the sun visor to see what damage had been done to my face. But he slapped my hand down, and closed it right back. "Don't touch a damn thing in my car! I don't care how messed up your face is."

As we approached a red light, uneasiness writhed in my gut. I was still feeling horrified of what extra he might do. Then I noticed a cop car pulling up on the side of us, and several thoughts raced through mind. Deep down inside, I really wanted to jump out as soon as the car came to a stop. I wanted to beg the cop for help, but fear had me trapped and confused. Something needed to be done; I knew I couldn't go on like this.

I nervously eased my hand up to the car handle door, making an attempted to bust a move. But suddenly, there was a sharp pain in my left side. Something was poking in my waist. I was in even more shock a moment later, when I realized it was my husband holding a knife to me, warning me not to do anything irrational. His left hand was still on the wheel, as he looked straight ahead. His teeth were clenched, but I heard what he said perfectly. "If you even think about jumping out of this car, you will regret it and I promise you that."

My first thought was to just go ahead and jump out of the car, taking that jab to my side. But fear clung to me. There was a possibility that he could stab me in the wrong spot; he could kill me, and my children with grow up motherless. Or, he could permanently injure me, and I wouldn't be able to take care of my kids.

Before I knew it, the light turned green, and Bradley hit the gas. The cop made the first right after the light, taking any hope of my escape with him, and we continued to keep straight. I rested my face back in my hands, sighing deeply and praying that we make it back home to Cedar Park soon.

Then, out of nowhere, Bradley gives me another surprise blow to the back of my head, causing me to smash my nose on the dash board. "Don't you ever try to get me put in jail with that slick shit," he said in a calm voice. "If you ever think about putting me in jail, just know that I will be back out within a couple of hours to beat the living hell out of you again."

He continued to threaten me for several more miles, but I wasn't listening. I was only thinking about stopping the trickle of blood that oozed down my chin. I pinched my nose, letting my eyes gaze into the night sky. I caressed my swelling cheek, frowning pitifully, knowing it would be at least a week or so until I was able to come out of the house or have company coming over.

Chapter Two

The warm water spraying down onto my face as I sat inside the walk-in shower in the master bedroom was the best feeling ever. My best friend, Kalisha, stopped by thirty minutes earlier to pick up BJ and take him to the zoo, and before her arrival, I made sure to pile lots of Noxzema over my face, covering the bruises from the night before. Brielle fell asleep shortly after BJ left, so that meant I was able to get some me time until she woke up for another feeding.

I stayed in the shower longer than usual, enjoying sitting under the shower head, but my mind and my emotions were all over the place. Bradley dropped me and the kids off after the beating he'd giving me in the car, and he still hadn't come home yet. And not knowing what to do or where to go if I decided to leave him scared me; he was all I had and all I knew since I was eighteen. I had three years and two kids with him. He took care of us and made sure we never wanted for anything.

I allowed myself to finally cry, letting the water wash the tears from my face as they fell from my eyes. At this point I missed my mother so much; I would give anything to be in her arms. As for my little sister, London – it was unbearable, not knowing if she was okay or not. I wonder if she missed me, or if she ever even thought about me.

My thoughts drifted back at times when I was alone, back to my mother and sister. There wasn't a day that went by when I didn't think about the day of my high school graduation back in May 2000. I remember early that morning when London and I woke up, unable to find our mother. We searched for her in the house, calling for her. Then we walked into her bathroom to find her lifeless body lying on the side of the garden tub. A needle was stuck in her right arm, and her mouth was wide open. I remember seeing her eyes rolled in the back of her head.

I remember my body going into shock; I couldn't move at all, not even able to grab my sister into my arms as she fell to the floor. I watched as she shook my mother's limp body, screaming uncontrollably. So badly I wanted someone to pinch me so I could wake up from this bad dream, but reality didn't hit me until when the tall, slender Spanish detective was in our living room asking us all kinds of questions as they carried my mother out in a black body bag.

"Paris, sweetheart do you have any other family?" he asked. "Is your father around?"

I scoffed. Now, that was a definite no. I never knew mine or London's father. The only thing I knew is that my mom told me the day she was getting ready to leave from the hospital to go home after giving birth to me, my father never returned to take us home, and that was the last time she had ever seen him. Then, four years later she gave birth to London, and after that it was just the three of us, living happily in our four bedroom home in Pflugerville.

I still couldn't digest the fact that my mother died of a heroin overdose. There were never any signs of her using drugs; the woman never even smoked a cigarette. She would have a wine cooler every now and then, but that was the extent of it. My mother was beautiful – she had the type of beauty that belong in a fashion magazine or on a runway. Her long, jet black curls stopped halfway down her back, and she had candy yellow skin with a pair of honey hazel eyes to die for. Everyone said she resembled the eighties pop singer, Apollonia, or even Sheila E. It was a gift to have such a beautiful mother, but a curse as well. I never wanted her to come up to my school because there was always one or two teenaged boys who couldn't control their hormones. It made me sick whenever I would hear nonsense like, "Damn, your mom is fine," or "Are you sure that's not your older sister? She too fine to be your mom." My sister, London, and I looked so much like her, sometimes I wondered why guys would push me to the side the minute they saw my mom.

Life was great in our household; we would take family vacations three times a year. The house we lived in was in a middle class neighborhood in Pflugerville, and my mother made sure we had nice clothes to wear at all times. We didn't want for anything; she did everything herself as a single mother. Now, how she maintained all of that on a secretary's salary, I don't know, but she gave us the world. Which is why I could never wrap my head around this drug overdose thing; a single mother and drug addict would not have been able to give her kids what my mother gave us. And not only that, but the needle that was found in my mother's right arm made question marks dangle around in my head, considering that she was right handed. I knew she was horrible about doing things with her left hand.

Ms. Kathy, my best friend's mom, who was like a second mother to London and me, arrived the morning of my mother's death and hadn't left my side since. She was the sweetest thing ever – a person who would give you the shirt off of her back, but who also wouldn't hesitate to speak her mind whenever it was necessary. After the detective spoke with Ms. Kathy, handing her his card, she thanked him with tears in her eyes.

Then the detective turned to me and London with sympathy. "I'm very sorry about your mother," he said. "Contact me if you need anything."

All I could do was nod my head. Then, as I looked into his face, I saw something I hadn't noticed before. Ms. Kathy sat on the couch to cradle London in her arms, as they both cried. Everything to me is such blah, still in shocked, no tears, still hoping this was a horrible dream, and that somebody would shake me awake. Turning to walk to the couch, the back of my head starts to throb, I feel dizzy, my vision is dimmed, and weakness is what I feel in my body. I can't see Ms. Kathy or London, but I can hear their voices.

"Paris! Are you ok! " Was that last thing I heard, before hitting floor to black out.

Kalisha and Ms. Kathy stayed over with us until my mother was laid to rest, most of the time I would stay in bed with a bottle of over the counter sleeping pills. While in one of my deep sleeps, Ms. Kathy's said that a short middle aged oriental guy stopped by with some paper work stating that my mother's memorial service expense were taken care of, and that he would be back on the day of the funeral with a stretch limo to drive us to the funeral.

"Well, Corina did know a lot of rich people. So maybe one of her friends paid for everything. " Ms. Kathy stated as she prepared her famous smothered pork chops, with the sides of mac and cheese, and cabbage. I was really not in the mood to eat at all, scanning through the funeral service paper work and receipts that read Lake Tears Funeral Home at the top, and at the bottom it read $10,000 paid in full cash. Feeling confused and wondering who loved and cared for my mother so much, to where they paid for her funeral service. I looked over the receipts and paper work over and over, to see if I could catch a name or something. Accepting the blessing and being very grateful for it, considering that my mother never had a discussion about burial insurance and how important it is to have it, I'm not sure what we would have done without this anonymous person's help.

A dozen of strangers showed up to the funeral, claiming to be very good friends of my mother. Everyone seems to be dressed for a fashion show, decked out in Gucci and Armani.

"Who are all of these people?" London asked feeling very irritated as each person approached us with the same statement over and over.

"Sorry for your loss" "Your mother was a very beautiful sweet woman"

After the unfamiliar pallbearers carried my mother out to be laid into her grave, London and I decided to make our way to the limo so we could go home. Kalisha and Ms. Kathy waited for us inside; we had had enough of everything with all of these strangers, and not one family member we knew of in sight.

A week and three days go by, and I still haven't gotten use to not hearing my mother's voice, or not waking up to the smell of her cooking. Just as my feet hit the floor to get out of bed, a loud knock at the door causes me to jump. To my surprise an unfamiliar brown skinned woman with shoulder length straight hair, is at my door step with a two white Travis County Sheriff Officers holding blue and yellow documents in hand.

"Can I help you?" I asked still half asleep and annoyed.

"Hello, my name is Betty Andrews. I'm the Aunt of London Scott" She spoke properly.

Staring at the woman in disbelieves, frowning at her like this was a joke, and finally I spoke.

"What do you want?" I barked at her, knowing that some unwanted drama was about to take place. A fake smile appeared on her face, that I desperately wanted to slap off her face.

"Well, I understand that your mother just passed away. What I have here are documents stating in your mother's will, that if something was to ever happen to your mother Corina Scott, I would be the one to have full custody of my niece London Scott until she is eighteen years of age. I know this is a very difficult time, but all I want is to take my niece and go on. Stepping onto the porch making eye contact with the coffee stained teeth woman, I know my morning breath hit her unexpectedly.

"Woman you must be out of your cotton picking mind, if you think I'm about to let you take my sister away! Get your raggedy ass off my doorstep! Now! " Now screaming at the top of my lungs, closer to her face. One of the officers stepped in between us, facing me while the other pulled her to the side.

"Ma'am please cooperate and let Mrs. Andrews take her niece home."

"This is her home! She has no right! Why are you here? Where is her father? Why is he not the one that's here? " I yelled even more, but yet not getting too crazy with the officers.

"Ma'am pleases! Go and get your little sister, don't make us arrest you"

Stepping back, taking deep breaths at a time. I walked into London's room to explain to her about what was going on, and called Ms. Kathy to come over. She and Kalisha arrived within ten minutes from the next subdivision, asking the officers about what was going on.

"Ma'am, do you really have to take London away? I mean they just lost their mother for crying out loud. " Ms. Kathy pleaded with this Betty woman, who showed no once of sympathy at all. The only look that she wore on her face was an; "I don't give a damn look." Seeing that all the pleading and begging this woman wasn't going to change anything, London and I embraced each other the whole time in tears while Ms. Kathy and Kalisha place her bags in the trunk of the gold Mercedes, the Betty woman sat back leaning up against her car with a smile on her face.

"London, as soon as you can, please call me. You have my cell number; I will always be here for you no matter what. " I told her, as I took off one of my gold bangles and place it on her left wrist. " London, please make sure you call me. "

"I promise to call you Paris, I love you" Crying her little heart out, as she gets into the car.

"I love you to London." I replied back, turning to walking away not wanting to see her go. "Oh by the way, since you think I'm out of my cotton picking mind. Tomorrow by 5pm you will need to vacate the property, and I will need the keys to the White Lexus and the Black

Tahoe. " She says with a bigger smile on her face, and the other officer handing me an eviction notice.

"Those are my mother's vehicles! I'm not giving you a damn thing! " I yelled charging at her, with a closed fist, and Ms. Kathy and Kalisha pulling me away.

"Little girl, there is a lot you don't know about your high yellow mammy, don't nothing belong to her or you. Now go get my damn keys so my niece and I can leave, you got some packing to do my darling. "

"Ma'am if know where the keys are in the house please go and get them so we can go"

One of the officers said noticing he was getting fed up with me and this woman going at it.

After handing over both sets of key to the officer, slamming the door. Running into my mother's bedroom to jump in her bed, screaming and crying uncontrollably as I squeezed the pillows tight, taking in her scent. The first time in my life I didn't realize how strong my lungs were until now; this was all too much for me. At this moment I didn't want to be on earth anymore, what did I have to live for? The two people who meant the world to me were gone, just like that within a blink of an eye.

Ms. Kathy took me in after all of the drama was over with, the only thing I had left was my Royal Blue 1998 Honda Civic that my mom purchased for me on my sixteenth birthday. The only reason why that wasn't taking away from me is because my mom had the title in my name and it was paid for in cash. I took up a job as a CNA at nursing home in North Austin, and then Kalisha and I both enrolled into the community college for nursing school. Considering what had all just taken place, I was on traveling down the right road. On my way to success to making something out of myself. Until I took a detour in February 2001, during one of Texas worst ice storm. Walking into the Auto Shop that was located in walking distance near my job at the nursing home. Praying that my heater was fix and ready to go, I was not able to take another day driving in the cold without heat.

"Excuse Me Sir, I'm here to see if the 98 Honda is ready" Approaching the nice looking slender well-built gentleman dressed in the all blue jumper, sitting behind the desk reading a VIBE Magazine. Once tossing the book to the side, his cinnamon brown complexion and full lips caused my eyes to stay glued to him. He was sexy as hell; his smile reminded me of Colgate toothpaste commercial.

"What's the owner's name of the vehicle?" He asked making eye contact, with a slight smirk on his gorgeous face.

"Paris Scott." Replying back trying my best not to blush.

"Yep! It's ready to go, it's parked out front" he stated handing me the keys.

"Ok, how much do I owe you?" Digging in my purse for my wallet.

"Dinner and a movie"

"What! Boy you crazy as hell" I barked at him

"No I meant let me take you out, and get to know you."

"Are you serious?"

"Yes, here is my card. My cell and work number is on it"

Damn, his smile drove me crazy, and he was bold. I liked that, my little young behind was all smiles, and speechless.

"So, what's your name?" Noticing he was not wearing a name tag.

"My name is on the business card that I just gave you"

"Cocky Bastard" saying to myself as I took another look at the card that read Frost Auto Shop, Owner Bradley Frost.

I agreed to meet him at the Cheesecake Factory for our first date; he was so sweet I instantly fell for him within a split second. We continued to date, and hang out every other day. We even went away for long weekends out of town; this was the first time in almost a year that I have had happiness. He was something new and exciting; I never had any man to be so sweet to me. Two months into our relationship, I discovered that I was pregnant with BJ. Bradley made it clear that if I was having his child then he wanted his family together. Meaning under the same roof, right at that moment I knew breaking the news to Ms. Kathy was going to be like pulling teeth. Even though I was eighteen years of age and I could leave whenever I wanted, but deep down inside I knew Ms. Kathy wanted the best for me, and she was doing what my mother would have wanted.

"Baby, I'm telling you. Please don't move out with that boy. Him and his family are all criminal minded and sooner than later you will sucked into some mess. Please Paris! Just stay here and I will help you raise the baby so you can finish Nursing School. "

Ms. Kathy begged and pleaded with me over and over as I placed my Purple Adidas Gym Bag in the trunk of my car.

"Ms. Kathy he is not like that, I love him and he loves me, and we are going to be family. Mama Kathy just please be happy for me."

Taking me into her arms with tears, sadden my heart, especially when I notice Kalisha sitting on the porch crying.

"Sweetheart, I can't say that I am happy about this, but what I can do is leave your room open to come back whenever you need to. I'm here for you and the baby. "

After kissing Ms. Kathy good bye, I was making my way over to Kalisha to give her my good byes, but she got up to go inside the house; giving me a pissed off look. As I made a note in my head to call her in a couple of days after everything has calmed down, I proceeded out of the drive way in more tears. On my way to Bradley's North West Austin Townhome, my new home with my man, and whoever wasn't happy for me. Then they could kiss where the sun don't shine.

Nervously walking into the double glass doors of Bradley's parents Westlake Hills Mansion Home, taking me to meet his parents for the first time. So amazed at how beautiful the home was I couldn't keep my eyes off of the Swans and ducks located in the little build in pound area. The front entrance of the home reminded me of a luxury hotel lobby, with fine art hanging on the wall. To my surprise a short petite salt and pepper gray headed woman with a thick accent appeared out of nowhere, wearing a black and white dress maid uniform.

"Hello Bradley! Your Parent's are in the living room. "

"Thank you Ms. Marry. This is my fiancé Paris, and Paris this is Ms. Marry, My Parent's Housekeeper. "

We shook hands, and then made our way into the living room area. Mrs. Frost immediately walked over to me with her arms open, in her all white mini dress and hot red stiletto heels. Right off the back I could tell that this woman had style and class, she looked to be just a little bit older than I was, but not old enough to be a mother of a twenty three year man.

"It's nice to meet you, how's my grand baby!" She said rubbing my pudgy stomach.

"Having me sick as a dog every morning" I replied laughing.

Mr. Frost approached us, standing in front of me with a glass of vodka in hand. Looking very handsome, as his well-built frame displayed through his all white V-neck Armani. It was obvious that Bradley inherent his good looks.

"Hello Mr. Frost, it's finally nice to meet you"
Extending my hand for a hand shake.

Taking a sip of his vodka, shooting me a nasty look. He walked away without saying a word, leaving me hanging without a hand shake. The next day Mr. Frost called Bradley ranting and raving about how we shouldn't get married, and that I needed to get an abortion. The whole thing seemed so weird; in this type of situation it was usually the mother who acted a donkey behind her son. I could not figure out for the life of me, why Mr. Frost instantly hated my guts since day one and I haven't even met the man a day in my life. After days of Bradley and his father going back and forth with each other, we decided to fly out to Las Vegas and that's when I went from Paris Scott to Paris Frost. We had a private wedding ceremony at the Bellagio Hotel. Everything felt so right, I was floating on cloud nine, this was one of the happiest moments of my life. Until Bradley's phone on the table started to ring twice and then hang up, distracting me from dropping my robe to the floor so I could make my way into the shower with Bradley. I waited for it to ring again, same thing ring two times then hang up. Thinking to myself why would his friends or family be calling; knowing that we were on our honeymoon. Dialing the missed call number back, with an answer after three rings. I was starting to think that the person on the other end had the wrong number, with the sound of a crying woman's voice.

"Hello!"

"Who is this?"

"You called my husband's phone, who is this?"

"This is Bradley's baby mama, I am in labor and I need to talk to him now"

Instantly my blood was boiling like a pot of neck bones, I know that I just did not here her say "Bradley's Baby Mama" Speechless is what I am, my heart sitting at the bottom of my stomach, mouth wide open in shock.

"What the hell did you just say?"

"Look Wifey! I don't have time to play games on the phone! Tell Bradley that my water broke and the baby is coming! "

The minute she hung up, I was busting through the bathroom door screaming and cursing at Bradley as he was stepping out of the shower.

"You triflin bastard! What is this about some girl is having your baby! This is our wedding day! How could you do this to me! " Throwing the phone at his head, as he slipped into his black Calvin Klein Boxers. Reaching for the hair dryer to be the next item to throw at him, within seconds his hands were gripped around my neck. Flinging my body around like a rag doll all over the hotel suite.

"Girl don't you ever in your life throw shit at me, what the hell is wrong with you!"

Screaming into my ear so loud, I was afraid for my ear drums.

"Bradley let me go! You are gonna hurt the baby! " Crying out to him.

Just as we both hit the floor, falling over a chair, as I gasp for air. Trying my best to crawl away from him, hoping and praying that no harm will be done to my unborn baby. Crawling behind the couch, my body is yanked backwards, with painful carpet burns on my butt and back. Kicking and screaming, dragging me by my hair.

"Bradley Baby I'm sorry! Let me go! " I yelled even louder.

When he kicked open the double patio doors, the sun shining into the room. My mind went back to the scene of the movie The Five Heartbeats, when Big Red held the guy over the balcony. I just knew right then and there my life was about to be over with, and the words of Ms. Kathy crept back into my head when she tried to warn me about Bradley.

"Let me go! Bradley you are gonna hurt the baby! " Kicking harder as he rolled me out, locking the double doors, with me outside on the patio wearing nothing but my pink bra, and pink lace panties. Banging on the double doors screaming for him to let me back in, as the lights flashes up from the tourists cameras as they were being entertained seeing me practically naked. Just as I yelled out over the patio to the crowd "Help! Someone Is Trying To Kill ME! " Bradley jerked me back inside.

"Paris, I promise you that is not my baby! My ex has been trying to get back with me ever since you and I got together, she is lying sweetheart you have got to believe me" He pleaded with me as we both sat on the bed, me still in tears.

I wanted to believe him, hell I wanted to erase the whole episode out of my head. I felt like it was too late for me to run, I was already three months pregnant, and we were married. I couldn't walk away from all of this, what was going to happen to me if I left, what was next for me. We continued to have our ups and downs, as we proceeded with our marriage, then came three years later our baby girl Brielle Monique Frost. I gave her my sister's middle name for her first name. Bradley was cool with it, just as long as her name started with the letter B. Just like all the controlling Frost men wanted.

Chapter Three

Laying in the comfortable plush king-size bed, watching Brielle smile in her sleep made my heart melt. I would always hear about the saying: if a baby smiles in their sleep that meant angels were playing with them. Well, maybe it was my mother making her smile in her sleep. Turning my attention to the clock that read 8:45 pm, when hearing the front door shut. Bradley made his way into the bedroom after being gone for three days and me not knowing his whereabouts, made me ache inside not knowing what he was doing or who he was with. He didn't care at all, he would always inform me that he was the one making the money, paying the bills, and taking care of us. So my job was to shut up, look pretty, stay in my lane, and play my role as a wife and mother.

The last time I questioned him about his whereabouts when coming in at 4am, he dragged me out of bed, into the garage, throwing me into the back of our family Lincoln Navigator, and placing the childproof locks on so I couldn't get out. 15 minutes of me screaming at the top of my lungs, he came back to let me out because BJ woke up crying for me. Ever since then I never bother him that much.

"Where's BJ?" he asked, kissing Brielle on her cheek. She was still smiling in her sleep.

"He's asleep." I said dryly. "He had a long day with Kalisha at the zoo." I get up, walking into the bathroom, and hear a knock at the door.

"Are you expecting company?" he asked sarcastically with a smirk. I ignored him, though.

Moments later, though, as I turn off the water faucet from washing my hands, I hear the sound of two men conversing outside the door. I opened the bedroom door, pretending like I was going to the kitchen. To my surprise standing in the front entrance of the doorway, Bradley and his estranged brother Bryce, who just popped up out of nowhere. His frown turned into a more relaxed expression as I walked out, I could tell the conversation between the two of them was pretty heated and neither one of them seemed to be pleasant with one another.

"Hi Paris! Sorry to interrupt, I won't be long at all" Bryce smiled at me, but his smile faded away when he hit me with the unexpected question.

"What happened to your face?"

"Um, I fell down the stairs," I replied back with a quick made up lie, feeling embarrassed that I forgot that the bruises on my face were still in the process of healing. I turned to walk always, regretting that I even came out of the room.

"Yeah! Bradley, remember when mom always used to accidentally fall down the stairs?" He said to Bradley, making invisible quotation marks in the air with his fingers. This pissed Bradley off.

"Look," he said. "You need to go talk to dad about whatever agreement the two of you had with each other. I had nothing to do with that, now get the hell out of my house and don't ever come back again!"

Bryce didn't budge at all, standing there with a mischievous smile on his face. He seemed to be enjoying the fact that he was getting under his big brother's skin, which was not good on my end because after he was gone, that only meant Bradley was going to take it out on me violently or sexually. Either way I didn't have the energy or strength for either one, so it was really time for Bryce to get his ass on somewhere, because he was now starting to piss me off. This brother of his was not backing down for nothing in the world; something was telling me that he was here for a damn good reason. Trouble was around the corner, I could feel it, and this dude was not playing at all.

"Pops and I never had no damn agreement! Both of you got me caught up in the mess that the two of you had going on, I didn't ask for this! Now just to let you know, I spent four years locked up. So all of that barking you doing doesn't move me at all. You just like your old man, all bark but no bite but won't hesitate to raise a closed fit to a woman. You are just like dad, a coward, a sorry excuse for a man. I see you inherited his wicked ways."

It was something about Bryce that I somewhat admired. Judging from his whole demeanor and vibe, I could tell that life had already thrown him a curve ball and had bit him in the ass all at once, and was ready for whatever was about to come his way. Whatever was going on with him, his brother, and father was some serious trouble that was about to hit the fan.

Pulling into the driveway of Ms. Kathy's home made me realize how much I missed her and Kalisha. She called saying that she was cooking dinner, and she wanted to see the kids. Since Kalisha hadn't had any kids yet, Ms. Kathy loved and treated my kids just as if they were her own flesh and blood.

"I don't know why you just won't use your key, the locks were never changed," she said, playfully fussing at me as she took Brielle out of my arms when answering the door. The house still had the same warm cozy feeling, and the smell of fried chicken and greens floating in the air. Gosh I missed her cooking so much.

"Baby, I want to talk to you," she said seriously. "Let's take the kids up to Kalisha."

Doing as I was told, I made my way back down to sit on the porch with Ms. Kathy's, and her famous lemonade. Wondering what she needed to talk to me about.

"How's it going Mama Kathy?" Nervousness came over me.

"Well, I'm fine. The question is how you are doing?" she asked, looking me straight in the eye with a serious look on her face.

"I'm doing fine," I lied.

"Well, Paris. I'm not sure how well you know this husband of yours, I mean you only knew the man for two months then boom you were pregnant. However, I'm not going to get into that. You know I got promoted to be the head nurse at the Children's Hospital. Last night a couple brought their son to the emergency room because he was jumping off the stairs at home. The little boy had to get stitches in his forehead. When I came in the room to check the little boy out, the mother of the child was laying in her husband's arms crying her eyes out. Well, then again I can't say it was her husband, because you know why?"

Feeling very annoyed, not knowing what was the purpose of this long drawn out emergency room story, and I answered back. "No, why Mama Kathy?"

"Because it was Bradley holding the woman in his arms," she said. "He's married to you, so I'm wondering why in the hell he was there with this woman when he has a family at home."

Trying my best not to show any type of reaction, I was stunned. All I could do is think back to our wedding night three years ago, when some broad called Bradley's phone talking about she was in labor. "Mama Kathy, how old was this little boy?"

"He might have been a little bit older than BJ, his name on his chart read Brandon Frost. I don't think Bradley recognized me when I walked in the room, considering I have only met him once, which is fine with me, but I do remember him. Not only that his name is and other information was listed in his chart."

I was so upset by the unwanted news; I wasn't able to finish my Sunday Dinner that Ms. Kathy cooked. As soon as BJ finished up his food I packed up the kids so fast to get home so I could have a talk with Bradley, this was too much to deal with.

More anger came over me when pulling into the garage, and not seeing Bradley's truck, my head throbbing a hundred miles per hour, the palms of my hands sweating like crazy. Within minutes my silver BMW was pushing eighty-five miles per hour on the freeway, making my way to Westlake over to Frost's house. Thank God Mrs. Frost answered the door, happy to see her grandchildren.

"Well, hello my babies, what a surprise. Come on in!" All cheerful and happy like always.

"Mrs. Frost, I'm sorry to drop by without calling, but could you please watch the kids for me, something came up," I explain, trying my best not to wear my feelings on my face.

"Of course you can," she said. "I'm not doing anything."

Making my way back to the house, still no Bradley in sight. Remembering the time when I picked my mother's lock on her bedroom door to borrow her Jimmy Choo Pumps without her permission gave me a big bright idea. After getting two hairpins out of the bathroom, I worked my magic to the door knob of Bradley's office. Once the door popped open, I was on a mission. Anything and everything I could find with some type of bank statement information and account number, or some cash laying around would do me and the kids just fine if I decided to pack up the kids and leave.

With my luck of not coming across anything, and not knowing where to turn to next had me frustrated. Hearing the sound of the garage door open and close scaring the crap out of me, I manage to have everything put back, and out of the office before Bradley made his way around the corner. Walking into the kitchen, grabbing bottled water out of the refrigerator Bradley called out my name.

"Paris! Where are the kids?" Walking in the kitchen wearing an all-black jogging suit and a look of confusion on his face. Carrying two large stuffed animal teddy bears, one pink and the other one blue. "He has never brought anything home for the kids," I think to myself.

"I'm about to go pick them up from your mother's house," I said, taking a swig of my water.

"Well, why aren't they with you?" he asked, placing the bears to the side and looking at me with suspicion.

"I had some things to do, so I just dropped them off for a little while." Walking down the hall, I grab my purse and keys.

"Paris! Get your ass back over here right now!"

"Bradley don't start with me," I warn him. "I am not in the mood to fight with you tonight!"

As I continued walking to the door, not even able to get my hand around the doorknob. Out of nowhere, my feet were not touching the floor anymore, and a tight grip was formed around my neck by Bradley's bare hands, with my body slamming up against the wall, causing some type of object to fall on top of my head. When the sound of glass shattering onto the floor informed me that it was our wedding picture into pieces.

"Paris I don't know why you make me put my hands on you, but if I find out that you are up to anything, I'm going to snap your neck. Please do not make our children orphans."

Kicking and squirming, not able to scream or cry, with Bradley trying his best to choke the life out of me. I manage to dig my pink cotton candy manicure into his face, trying my best to go for his eyeballs. His grip gets tighter and tighter, as the tear falling from my left eye, his grip starts to loosen up. My body falls to the floor as he completely let's go, my body coughing and gasping for air, crawling away from him into a corner.

"Get up and go get my kids right now!" he barked at me.

I was not able to run out the door fast enough to get the hell away from him, it was really much needed for me to hurry up and think of some type of plan really quick, because if I stayed any longer Bradley would eventually kill me. The only time there was peace was when he was gone for days at a time, but not knowing where he was at. This was no way to live at all, and a good example could not be set for my kids by living this way. At this point regret from not listening to Ms. Kathy's words was knocking at my door.

Chapter Four

Talking to Bradley in the doorway of his office, he ignores me as he places a stack of hundred dollar bills into the money counter machine. After each count he continues to do the same with all of the other stacks that sit on top of his desk, and the others located on the floor next to a black gym bag filled with kilos of cocaine.

"Bradley, please hear me out. Kalisha wants me and the kids to take a trip to Florida at the end of this summer; it will only be for a few days."

"No the hell it won't be for no few days, because you are not taking my kids nowhere," he said. "If I want to take my family on a vacation then I myself will do it, not Kalisha. Now get out of my office so I can finish counting my money."

Storming off and feeling irritated, I hear the doorbell ring. It's my father-in-law. "Hello Mr. Frost. How are you?" I greeted him with a forced smile, wondering what the hell he wanted. His old mean behind never came over to the house.

"Where is my son?' he growled brushing right past me, not even acknowledging me in my own house. The disrespect was getting very old and tiring.

"Mr. Frost! I spoke to you and I would appreciate a little respect in my house!" I said, walking behind him trying to get his attention.

He whipped around so fast I had to take a few steps back. "Little girl, I don't have to respect you," he said." As far as I'm concerned, you are just another little young piece of ass that my son got caught up with. You are no different from the others. Now if you know what's best for you, you better get out of my face!"

"Hey! What's going on?" Bradley came walking down the hall. I rushed up to him indignantly, noticing him carrying the black gym bag.

"Bradley! I am so sick and tired of your father disrespecting me!" I yell at the top of my lungs in anger.

"Son, put a leash on this flea bag so we can get the hell out of here," he said coldly. "We need to go meet up with the Lopez family. It's too much money to be made, and I don't have time to sit here and argue with this thing you call your wife!"

My mouth dropped to the floor, I could not believe what just came out of his mouth. "Dad! Don't call her that, she is my wife, and the mother of your grandchildren. You have to respect her. Do not ever call her out of her name again!"

Standing there, I had to do a double take to make sure that it was my husband's voice that I was hearing. Not sure what came over him, this was the first time in three years that Bradley has ever stood up to his father in my defense.

"Son, if that's the case then I will never step foot in your house again, and she is no longer welcome into my house as well. I will never have respect for her, and I will never like her. However, son you do need to remember what I have always taught you. Never let some skirt get in the way of your Franklins." he said, shooting the most evil look in my direction and taking the gym bag out of Bradley's hand walking out of the door. "I'll be in the car waiting until you are finished with Miss Bold and The Beautiful here."

As he made his way out of the door, I wanted to pick up one of the glass flower vases and throw it at the back of his head. "Bradley, I am so tired of everything. I want to just go; you can have all of this," I said, my face soaking wet with tears. "Just give me a divorce and let me go. *Please.*"

Taking my hand, pulling me into his arms and holding me as I continued to cry, he ran his fingers through my long curls, taking deep breaths, speaking so calm and casual. "Paris, you know I can't and will not give you a divorce. We both said till death do us part, and that is what it will be until one of us leaves this earth. Don't do anything stupid that you might regret, I would love for you to be here to see our son go off to college, and to see our daughter grow up and get married. If you even so much as speak the word divorce in this house again, I will see to it that soup and baby food will be your only options on the menu for the rest of your life, after your jaw is wired shut from me breaking it. Now please make sure you thaw out some ground beef, I want to have meat loaf tonight for dinner when I come home."

Then he gave me a peck on the cheek and walked out of the door, leaving me standing speechless. I can't believe my own husband would just threaten to break my jaw and then request meatloaf for dinner like it wasn't nothing. This guy had a heart made of icicles, and didn't give a damn about nothing or no one.

The house phone rung, which was something unusual, startled me to death. The only person who would ever called the house phone was Mrs. Frost if Bradley or I didn't answer our cell phones.

"Hello?" I answered the unfamiliar number on the caller ID.

"Hi, Paris," said a man's voice. "Is Bradley home?"

"Who is this?"

"This is Bryce, his brother. I can't get hold of him or my dad."

This dude was starting to scare me, I just could not figure out why was it after all these years this long lost brother pops up, and him and Bradley including their father were all acting as if they couldn't stand each other. This was way too weird for me. "Look Bryce, Bradley isn't home," I said, getting agitated.

"Ok, well tell him if he knows what's best for him, he needs to get at me or the next pop up visit won't be so pleasant," he said with a sharp tone.

Slamming the phone down, I ran upstairs to dress the kids so I could drop them off at Ms. Kathy's house. It was time for me to go out job hunting; I desperately needed to find a way to make a living if I had planned to step out on my own with two kids. Damn! I hated that I let Bradley talk me into quitting nursing school and my job at the nursing home, I'm pretty sure if I would have stayed there and in school I would have gotten promoted to a higher position by now making a decent amount of money.

In the middle of dressing BJ into his Ralph Lauren shirt and jeans, I noticed the big blue teddy bear in the corner and the pink one next to Brielle's crib. Still finding it to be very strange that Brad came dragging in 2 giant teddy bears, that were damn near bigger than me, saying they were for the kids. BJ didn't like bears, he was into comic books and superman, and Brielle was barely crawling. The bears might have scared her if she crawled in its direction. Just for a split second I had forgotten how much my baby boy was growing up, how he was very smart for his age, and was picking up on things.

"Mommy! You told me that boys are not supposed to hit girls, right?" he asked, sitting next to me on his race car bed, holding my hand as he played with my diamond wedding ring.

"That's right sweetie," I replied back to him.

"Then why does daddy hit you and make you cry?" he said, looking up at me with sadness in his eyes. It took everything in me to not burst into tears, and at the same time trying to recall which episode he had witnessed his father being in rage. After collecting my thoughts on how to explain Bradley's behavior to our three and a half year old son, finally I spoke.

"Baby, your dad has a problem and he needs help, mommy is going to try to get daddy some help and everything is going to be just fine."

"Well, I don't like it when daddy hurts you, and makes you have a bad boo on your face."

Bradley just doesn't know how much this was hurting like hell, trying to explain his actions to our son. I needed to get my kids and run like hell to another state. He had already made it clear that if I took the kids and left him, he would kill me. The messed up part about that is I knew that he would do it, so I really needed to figure out something. There was no need for me to have him put in jail, with all the money him and his father had. He would probably go in for a few hours and get right back out to hunt me down.

Feeling somewhat better and confident about the job interview I just walked out of at a North Austin OBGYN office for a Medical Administrative Assistant position, a huge smile was plastered across my face. Making an exit out of the double doors, a short brown skinned pregnant blond catches my attention. I noticed the weird look she was giving me. I pause for a minute, noticing the little boy she's walking hand in hand with carrying the same strong features as my son BJ. The only difference was that the little boy seemed to be a little older and taller than BJ, but the most noticeable feature that stood out on the boy was the scar on his forehead.

Never questioning Bradley about anything after having the conversation with Ms. Kathy about him being at the Children's Hospital with a woman and a little boy, made me want to drive straight to his office and go off. If I did that, then what would it solve? Bradley was still going to do whatever it was he wanted to do, and didn't give a damn how I or anyone felt about it.

Pulling up into the driveway noticing the smoky gray 2000 Buick Lesabre swangas and elbows parked across the street in front of Mrs. Woods two story house, made me do a double take. Nowhere here in Cedar Park a car like that would be spotted in a suburban community and especially in front of Mrs. Woods's house. An old Polish woman who would probably think someone was there to rob her, if she had ever seen a car like that in our neighborhood. To my surprise Bryce jumps out the car, walking over to my direction as I'm making my way into the house.

"Hey sister in-law! You know that was real fucked up for you to slam the phone down in my face, I really didn't deserve that. Your husband is already ducking and dodging me."

Now at this point I'm livid, this Bryce character is popping up out of nowhere and unannounced. What in the hell is it that he wanted from me, knowing damn well that his brother was not at home.

"Bryce, your brother is not here, and you know it, please leave." Trying my best to remain calm and not make a scene.

"I'm not leaving until I speak to him; I will sit here on your porch until he arrives home. Well, that's if he decides to come home tonight." He smirked just like his brother did when being sarcastic, now my blood was boiling like a pot of neck bones. Within a second or two I had kicked off one of my Pink Prada Pumps, and got to swinging it at him. His comment struck a nerve, and I wanted him to get the hell out of my sight.

"Get away from here you bastard!" Screaming at the top of my lungs, trying to hit him with the heel of my pump, as his slender frame jumped back every time I took a swing missing him by inches.

"You crazy ass girl! What's wrong with you!" Still jumping back, trying to miss the swing of my high heel shoe.

Coming close to hitting him, his block caused the heel to hit his arm. Then that's when he manages to snatch the shoe out of my hand, bear hugging me.

"Look woman, I'm not playing with you. Now calm your ass down!" he said, throwing me down onto the grass so hard, I rolled under the tree. His tall frame now standing over me, not knowing what he was going to do, I figured he wouldn't be crazy enough to give me a beat down in broad daylight in our neighborhood. Instead he grabs my ankle, snatching the other shoe off of my foot, and kneeling down to make eye contact.

"Now, that we just had a little scuffle, get up, go into the house and call your husband and tell him what just happened and I bet you his punk ass will be pulling up within minutes." he straightened out his shirt indignantly. "You see I'm nothing like my brother, I don't hit women. Now I advise you to take all that energy out on him and not me the next time you decide to hit someone with a high heel shoe."

Bradley made it home within 15 minutes after calling him to inform him of what just took place, his brother still sitting outside on the porch. He was heated and was ready to give Bryce what he had been asking for ever since he popped up out of the blue.

Bradley dragged Bryce into the house, with his 45 Special in hand.

"Didn't I tell you not to come back to my house? You keep dancing on my nerves, bro!" he said. "Please don't make me have to buy mama that black dress. I'm begging you!"

Standing there watching my husband about to splatter his brother's brains out, aiming the gun in his direction. Bryce didn't budge at all. Instead he walked right up to Bradley, with his chest now touching the gun.

"You either kill me right here, or put the gun down and fight me like a man. Really I don't think you got the balls to do either one." He spoke to his big brother with a straight face.

"Bryce! I'm not playing with you, get the hell out of my house, and don't ever come back again!"

My feet cannot move; I'm in shock. What if my husband pulls the trigger, right here and right now? God please turn this situation in a different direction, I pray quietly to myself.

Bryce moved a couple of steps back, not taking his eyes off of Bradley and the gun.

"Don't think that this is going to make me go away, you and punk ass pops still need to be a man of your word. I'm gonna get my money or way or another Big Bro!"

A huge weight was lifted off my shoulders when Bryce walked out the door. My nerves were in shock, and my emotions now all over the place; this was too much. My body flops onto the living room couch, in tears like always. I have never cried so much in my life until I married Bradley. My eyes stayed bloodshot red for days at a time, the whole three years. Bradley walked over, placing the gun onto the coffee table, sitting down next to me on the couch. Pulling my whole body on top of his, holding me the same way he held Brielle. Something he hadn't done in a very long time since we first started dating. This was the part I missed so much about him. I loved and missed the way he used to hold me in his arms, and talk to me. "Sweetheart, I know that I haven't been the best husband, but please know that I am trying. I never meant to bring any type of harm your way. You have been through hell and back since your mother passed away, then your little sister getting taken away right after that and still not knowing her whereabouts. I want to change and be a better man for my family. Paris I love you and the kids so much, it scares me to lose the three of you. Just please bear with me sweetheart, and I promise to do right by you."

Damn those words sounded so good coming from him, it's like he changed back into the person I met three years ago. Why couldn't he just be this person 24/7? I prayed that things would work out and he would not go back to being the monster he was before.

Two months later I'm lying on top of the medical exam table, in Dr. Whitfield's office as she moves the monitor up and down, and across my belly. Informing me that I was three months pregnant. I looked over at Bradley, seeing the smile on his face was priceless. Things were going great for us, he was home more, there were no fights, and his dad and brother weren't popping up at the house causing drama. It felt so good to have my family back together. I was so happy.

Chapter Five

It's four in the morning and I'm jumping up out of my sleep to the loud banging sound at the door. At first I thought I was having a bad dream, but the red and blue lights flashing outside of the bedroom window quickly alerted me that I wasn't dreaming.

"Williamson County Police!" someone yelled from the hall. "GET ON THE GROUND! GET ON THE GROUND!"

My poor pregnant bladder couldn't hang, but pissing all over my yellow nightgown was the least of my worries. A group of officers had drawn their guns at us, pointing directly at my temple and at the back of my husband's head. There was no way for me to lay down on the floor with my belly in the way.

"Sir, I'm pregnant," I yelled. "I can't lie on my stomach!"

Thankfully, the officer was obliging. He made me sit in the corner instead, where I watched them handcuff Bradley and drag him off.

I was shaken, but I quickly remembered my babies. "Officer! I have a three year old, and an infant upstairs," I said. "Can I please go get them? I don't want them to wake up scared."

One of the men nodded and pulled me to my feet. "I'll walk you," he said.

Brielle had woken up, but BJ was still asleep. The officers let me stay in the kids' room while they searched our home for drugs and money. A middle aged, female officer with red hair came into the room with me and the kids. I halfway thought about throwing BJ's basketball piggy bank upside her head, when she started to search through the kid's dresser drawers. After not finding anything, she stepped into the hallway, talking to the other officers. The phone started to ring and the officer gestured for me to answer it. I wasn't even able to get a full hello out before Mrs. Frost's cries blared through the receiver. "OH MY GOD!" she yelled. "COPS ARE EVERYWHERE. THEY TORE UP OUR HOME; THEY TOOK BRADSHAW TO JAIL!"

Even though the same thing was happening to me in my own house, my heart still went out to Mrs. Frost. I felt so sorry for her. My body started to grow weak, my head throbbing, and my vision blurred. This feeling was all too familiar. This was the feeling I had the day my mother died. And even though I knew what was going to happen next, I wasn't prepared when my body hit the floor.

The clock on the wall read 3:15, but I wasn't sure if it was in the morning or afternoon. Slowly turning my head to right, I notice a monitor and an IV bag hanging above. To my left, I see Kalisha and Mrs. Frost both by my side with tears in their eyes.

"Oh God," I moaned. "What happened? Where are the kids?"

Mrs. Frost walked over to the side of the hospital bed, taking my hand into hers.

"The kids are with Ms. Kathy," she said. "You passed out when the cops came to arrest Bradley."

Trying my best to sit up, I falter. A sharp pain in my lower stomach would not allow me to. My hand reached down to feel the lower part of my stomach and I noticed that it wasn't big and bloated anymore. I started to panic in fear.

"WHERE IS MY BABY?" I cried out so loud that Kalisha jumped.

"Paris, Sweetheart, you lost the baby," said Mrs. Frost with tears in her eyes. Her voice cracked. "It was a girl. I am so sorry." Mrs. Frost cried even more.

I couldn't understand. Why was this happening to me? Haven't I already lost enough? The door opens with two knocks, Bryce walks in with sadness in his eyes. Just the bastard to see who probably had a hand in all of this mess. It's mighty strange how the domino effect started ever since he's popped up in the picture, just out of the blue. Walking over to his mother as she holds me in her arms, Mrs. Frost frees one arm to hug and kiss Bryce.

"Paris, I am so sorry, I know that I cannot change what happened, but if you need anything just know that I am here for you and the kids." Bryce spoke with sincerity, but I didn't feel it. The feeling I had was anger towards him, and very agitated with his presence. I wanted him to leave, not able to stand the sight of this rat bastard. Turning to lay back down, me still being on mute, not even wanting to look at him. The nurse enters the room to get my vitals, and to inform me of my doctor's orders. After the nurse walks out, Kalisha grabs her purse.

"Paris I am going to make my way back to the house, so my mom can leave out for her trip to New Orleans. I will do my best to clean up most of the mess that the cops left. I will be back tomorrow." She kissed me on my forehead, and then walked out the door.

Mrs. Frost begins to start thinking out loud, walking over to sit inside the large window sill biting her nails.

"I can't believe all of this is happening, I feel like a horrible mother, how could I allow Bradshaw to drag my son down in the gutter along with him."

Bryce shot his mother a nasty look, biting his bottom lip. "Mom, there are a lot of things I can't believe about your husband. At first I thought you knew what was going on and what has gone on in the past, but to come and find out you are just so blinded by the diamonds and handbags that he has constantly shoved in your face throughout the years. He has had you trained damn near all of your life to just shut up and look pretty, and if you did otherwise, he would be kicking your ass all up and down and around the house. There is so much more that you don't know about your husband and perfect son. If I sat here and told you everything, we would be here all night long."

Mrs. Frost stepped away from the window, walking in Bryce's direction.

"Now you listen, I am still your mother and you will respect me," she said. "Don't you ever talk to me like again, Bryce." She spoke with a sharp tone, pointing her perfectly manicured finger at him with a furrowed look on her face.

"How can you demand respect from me after all of these years?" said Bryce. "Growing up, you have allowed your husband to treat me like a red headed stepchild, showing favoritism with Bradley and I. Just because guilt was eating at your ass from having a child outside of your marriage doesn't mean it was ok for you to allow him to treat me the way he did." Mrs. Frost's mouth dropped to the floor, when Bryce spit out a mouth full right before her eyes. Then he continued on. "What's wrong, mom? Oh you didn't know that I knew about him not being my real father. Well, maybe you and your husband shouldn't have arguments with your bedroom door wide open, or maybe you should not have allowed him to always refer to me as your illegitimate bastard. So, yeah! I would hear the two of you arguing and fighting about the affair you had with his business partner Johnny Lopez. You got to remember mom, kids are like sponges, and they soak up everything and carry it with them and ring it out at the right time. So Mother, sorry for all of the water I just splashed in your face."

I guess this was all too much for Mrs. Frost to take in all of the skeleton bones that her son was throwing her way; she and I both wore blank stares with awkwardness floating through the air. Mrs. Frost grabbed her sunglasses and cell phone from the counter top, and then walked over to Bryce. Taking her arm reaching all the way back to Alabama, slapping the hell out of Bryce with tears rolling down her face. Bryce stood there in silence, and then gave his mom a mischievous smirk.

"Do you feel better mom?" He ask still wearing the smirk on his face, which I'm pretty sure pissed her off even more to where she stormed out of the hospital room not saying a word. For a minute I was kinda distracted from my own issues that just took place, a huge part of Mrs. Frost's dark past was brought to the light, and I was in the front row center to watch as the spotlight shined over her. Bryce turns to me, rubbing his left cheek.

"Considering what just took place with you, I should have had that outburst someplace else, and I am very sorry"

Taking deep breaths, trying to prepare myself for what I'm about to ask this rat snitching bum, that just might send him over the edge.

"Bryce, you might flip out on me after I ask you this question, frankly my dear I really don't give a damn. Considering I just lost my child, my husband is now locked up, and there is no telling when me or my kids will ever get to see him again. I just want to know one thing. Did you have anything to do with Bradley and your father getting busted? I find it to be very strange that you show up out of the blue, causing drama about money then before you know it my house is getting kicked in by Williamson County Police. My husband being hauled off to jail."

Bryce stares at me with disbelief for a split second, walking closer to me on the right side of the bed. The look of disbelief turns into an angry frown.

"If you were just listening to everything that I just revealed to my mother a second ago, you would know that Bradshaw Frost is not my father, I just wear the asshole's last name because of my mother's wrong-doing. Another thing I see is that you don't know much about your husband, you are just as gullible as my mother. Not having a clue at all none whatsoever, but before I leave without

53

cursing you out and telling you how I really feel about that garbage that just came out of your mouth. I will say this. I'm not a rat or snitch, and especially to my own family. Even though they did some rotten shit to me that I did not deserve, never in my life I would hand them over. Now I must leave before I step out of character and forget that you are lying up in this hospital bed, you just insulted the hell out of me.

Laying there as he turned away to leave out, wishing that I was able to jump out of this hospital bed and choke the life out of him. No one could tell me any different, or make me feel any different. I know that he snitched on my husband, and I wish that we would go back to wherever the hell he came from.

After Kalisha helped me get buckled into the car, so happy to be going home to my babies. Being away from them for three days, I missed them so much.

"Kalisha, before we go to the house, could we make one stop. I want to visit my mother"

"No problem. I'm going to be staying with you and the kids for a while if that's cool. I don't want to leave you just yet, everything is still fresh," she replied, rubbing my back.

I thank God for having Kalisha and Ms. Kathy in my life, they both have been in my corner since day one, even throughout the times of me making horrible decisions and being hard headed. The two of them have remained by my side with nothing but love and support.

"Wow! It's been a while since I have been out here," I thought to myself as we pulled into Lake Tears Cemetery.

"Paris do you want me to walk out there with you?"

"No, I'll be fine, thank you Kalisha," I said, getting out of the car.

"Ok Love, take as much time you need to take."

Standing in front of the big black beautiful gigantic headstone, in gold letters that read

"Corina Monique Scott March 20, 1967 - May 17, 2000"

Taking a deep breath, with tears, I began to speak with a heavy load on my heart and mind that was much needed for a release.

"Mom, I know that my baby girl arrived in heaven with you three days ago, and she is safe in your arms. You might not be happy with me right now as you look down on me from above. Everything that you have taught me in life, I have done the complete opposite. Mom, I am scared, I'm lost. God I would give anything to be in your arms to feel your warmth. Missing you so much it hurts. If my baby sister London is there in heaven with you, please let her know that I miss and love her so much. Take care of my baby girl, I love you mom."

Chapter Six

Strutting down the hall of Williamson County Courthouse, I passed by a number of lying, crooked lawyers and every set of eyeballs were on me. Sporting an all gray pants suit, along with my favorite cherry red pumps, my hair up in a French twist with china doll bangs. My appearance said that I was there to represent a client, but in reality I was there to meet up with my husband's lawyer to discuss his case. Six months had flown by so quickly since Bradley's arrest. Brielle was already trying to walk and BJ was in basketball camp and karate.

Our babies were growing up right before my eyes, and it hurt like hell that Bradley was missing out on everything. There was no telling how much more he was going to miss out on, because he was carrying some serious charges against him. I enter the office and my hands are shaking. There was an average height, husky all white hair lawyer, wearing an all-black suit with a black cowboy hat. His appearance reminded me of the old white man on the Quaker Oatmeal box. "Hello Paris," he greeted me with a thick good old country boy accent. "My name is Marshall Duncan. I'm going to be presenting your husband."

"Nice to meet you," I replied back, forcing a smile. Following him into a room with a long conference table, a tall slender black bald headed male wearing a light brown prison guard uniform standing at the end of the table. Shockingly Bradley sitting at the other end of the table, dressed in a dark blue jail scrub uniform. Fear and tiredness displayed on his face, his facial hair that had grown out almost into a beard made him look like he aged a full decade within six months since the last time I had seen him during his arrest. Even though Bradley has put me through so much hell it was crazy how I still had a soft stop for him in my heart, I still loved him and sometimes I hated that feeling that I had for him. What was I to do? He was still my husband and the father of my kids, and I couldn't just leave him to rot in jail like it wasn't nothing. Standing to his feet with his hands cuffed in front of him, within seconds I made my way over to him wrapping my arms around him, placing kisses all over his face then onto his lips. I almost forgot the guard was standing at the end of the table, so I backed off a little not wanting him to say anything. Using both cuffed hands to lift up my face by my chin, making eye contact with each other.

"Baby, I want to say that I am so sorry for putting you and the kids through so much, and the loss of our baby girl. You just don't know how much it hurts me."

As I wiped away the tear drop falling from his eye, kissing him one more time before Mr. Duncan asked us to start the meeting.

"Ok Bradley, this is the deal here. They really want your father; the DEA wants to make you an offer that can give you a less time. With all of the evidence they have on both of you, you are looking at very long prison sentences."

"What are they offering?" Bradley anxiously asked, looking straight ahead at his lawyer without a blink. Mr. Duncan shifted back and forth in his chair, seeming to be very uncomfortable to deliver whatever it was.

"Bradley, the DEA wants you to testify against your father. They have been wanting to get him for years now, way before you were even born. He has beaten every single case. I have to go meet with another client, but this is something that you really need to think long and hard about." Mr. Duncan stated.

"I'm not no damn snitch, you must be crazy to think I'm gonna rat on my father. What the hell I'm paying you for?" Bryce volume went up a tab bit, but calmed down when realizing where he was as I started to rub his arm.

"You are not hearing me. You could be gone for a very long time to where you might not get to see your children graduate, and another thing. I might be out of order for saying this, but you might want to find out the real reason why your brother Bryce went away. When I come back tell me how you feel after you have sat and marinated on everything that I just brought to your attention. Have a good day Paris; call if you have any other questions."

He picked up his briefcase, placing his hat back on top of his head walking out the door, with the guard coming back in to take Bradley back.

"Frost, time to go." The corrections officer spoke in a stern volume.

"Sir, could I please have just five more minutes to talk with my husband? Please?"

I begged with a slight pout in my full lips, batting my long Diana Ross eye lashes at him, hoping that would somewhat soften his heart. He looked at me with a slight grin, and then agreed. "Okay five more minutes, then I have to take him back."

After I thanked the officer, I immediately turned to my husband.

"Why are they doing this Bradley? The cops didn't find anything when they raided the house, why are you being charged with anything?" Trying my best not to cry.

"Paris, they tapped the phones at the Auto shop and the real estate office. When they raided the office, kilos of cocaine were found stacked in the locked file cabinets, money found in the built in wall safe. They even locked down my Auto shop, and it wasn't even anything there that they found. Somebody inside our circle has been feeding these pigs information; they went to all the stashes. Hell they even located some of our rental property finding more dope stashed there, but they never touched the other property that's located in South Austin. Whoever has been giving them information about me and my father is not enough; they want more so that's why they want me to snitch. They have everybody in custody at this moment; even my aunt B is in custody."

"Your aunt who?" I was confused.

"My aunt B. You never met her before; all of the property that we have under Frost Real Estate is in her name, even my Auto Shop and the office itself. She would do runs for us and drop off money, and keep her eye on the females who did work for my dad. I guess they offered her the same deal to snitch on my dad, but she refused to turn on her brother." Bryce really couldn't tell me every single detail within five minutes, the guard came back in to let us know that our time was up. Right before I walked out, Bradley called out to me.

"Paris, get my two Nautica Jackets at the back of the walk-in closet, cut the hood of them off, it will benefit you and the kids. Please just know I'm telling you this for a reason."

Looking at my husband as if he didn't have all of his marbles, I walked out of the door making my way to the parking feeling overwhelmed and frustrated. Scared and confused, not knowing what was next.

Pulling out my phone to give Kalisha a call, it was a must for us to have a girl's night out. A drink or two in my life was much needed right about now; I needed to relieve some stress. "Hey, let's check out that new club Liquid City, the grand opening is tonight." Kalisha said with full excitement in her voice.

"Okay, meet me at my house around seven tonight so we can roll out together, you might need to be the designated driver because I plan on getting tore the hell up" I replied back as we both busted out laughing.

Taking another look at my mint green mini dress in the mirror, I decided that the crush diamond stiletto heels that I haven't gotten a chance to wear would look better with my outfit. Reaching for the shoe box located at the top shelf, the two Nautica Jackets in the far back caught my attention. Reminding me of the craziest instructions Bradley gave me to before leaving the courthouse. It was not possible for me to ignore it; no matter how stupid it sounds I know he was telling me to do it for a damn good reason. Laying both jackets on top of the bed, grabbing the pair of scissors, feeling so stupid about to cut up two name brand jackets that still had the price tags on it. I proceeded to do just what my husband instructed. Removing the chopped off hood of the jacket, taking the other part to shake it. Scaring the hell out of me ten bundles of $100 dollar bills fall out onto the floor, dropping on top of my feet causing me to jump back. I couldn't believe my eyes, this couldn't be. I did the same with the other jacket. Another ten bundles falling out, a brown band wrapped around each bundle that read $5,000. That damn husband of mine is so clever, I guess he had the money stuffed inside the jackets, and sewed up by the cleaners. Just in case anything happened, the kids and I will be taken care of financially. Sitting on the side of the bed, in a daze staring at all the bundles of money on the bed. A knock is at the door, causing me to snap out of it.

Damn! I forgot Kalisha was on her way, so we could ride out to the club, throwing all of 20 bundles into my purple Adidas Gym Bag which added up to be 100,000 Grand. I took out one bundle placing it into my purse, to head out for girls' night.

All eyes were on us, stepping into Club Liquid City. Kalisha is wearing an all-white mini skirt and strapless top, with ocean blue pumps. My mint green mini dress caught everyone's attention. We both looked like The Black Barbie Twins, with our long curls flowing with the attention being all on us. I could see the hate in the females' eyes, as their nose turned up and eyes rolled in the back of their heads. The DJ was doing his thing as he played one of my favorites by UGK ``Let Me See It.'' Damn I loved the sound of Pimp C's voice over the speakers. The bartender handed Kalisha her Long Island Iced Tea, then handing me my Sex on the Beach Drink. My mind was at ease; I was feeling the relaxation after getting down to a quarter of my drink. Ordering another one enjoying the vibe, Kalisha spotted Jermaine West. A tall slender dark complexioned basketball player who we went to school with. He had the cutest smile, all pure white teeth. As fine as he was, I know damn well he wasn't in here by himself, his girl had to be somewhere around.

"Well if it isn't double trouble, Paris Scott and Kalisha White!" Jermaine approached us with friendly hugs. Not bothering to correct him on my last name now being Frost, it was kinda funny to hear Scott. Kalisha and Jermaine carried a long conversation over the loud music, I was happy to see her smile; I wanted her to meet someone. Just when I turned my head to the left, a weird feeling came over me when spotting the short blond headed girl walking through the crowd. I remember coming across her when leaving the OBGYN office from an interview, I noticed she wasn't pregnant anymore. The same crazy look she gave me the last time I saw her, was the same look she was giving me walking in my direction. Standing in front of me, with her arms folded wearing a black spaghetti strapped dress. Something was telling me that I was gonna have to whoop her ass, the way she was mugging me up and down.

"Is there a problem?" I barked at her.

"Yeah, you walking on this earth breathing is my damn problem. I hope Bradley knows his whore of a wife is out spending his money, while I'm left to struggle with two of his kids." At that moment all I could see was red, as those words rolled off of her lips. My second drink that I didn't even get to take a sip out of was in her face, breaking the drinking glass upside her head. My intentions were to smash the glass on the side of her face. A crowd formed around us when she fell to the floor screaming, holding the side of her head. Just when I was about to start stomping on her face with my high heels, my feet were no longer touching the floor. A man's bear hug grip was so tight around me, I could not move. I noticed that the bouncers carried her out the front door. For some reason I was being carried to the back, with the sound of Kalisha's voice screaming.

"Bryce put her down, let her go, that tramp came in here starting mess with her."

"Did she just say Bryce?" I had to ask myself. As soon as my feet touched the floor, whipping my body around to see who in the hell was carrying me.

"Well, I'll be damned. What in the hell are you doing here Bryce?" I yelled as we stood inside of the club's office. Noticing the all black Armani Suit he was sporting, he looked like he belonged in The Hamptons. The huge picture of him dressed in all white hanging above the desk caught my attention. Turning to him with a frown.

"What the hell is going on, why did you bring me back here?" Yelling at him.

"Relax! I wasn't going to let my bouncers throw you outside!" He yelled back.

"What the hell do you mean? You're Bouncers?"

"This is my club, tonight is the Grand Opening, and I wasn't about to let you and that hood rat tear up my club on the first night" He barked louder.

I didn't know this asshole was capable of running a business, when and where did he get the money to open up a club. Walking in Kalisha's direction to tell her that I was ready to go, Bryce took me by the hand.

"Paris, can I please talk to you?"

"No! I am going home! This is all too much, that whore just informed me that she has two kids by my husband, and now I'm sitting here face to face with the rat that put my husband behind bars! I hate you!" Running up to Bryce, constantly hitting him in his chest and arms, as hard as I can with my closed fist. He stands there in silence not making one move, staring at me like I was a mad woman. Kalisha grabs me from behind, trying her best to pull me away. "Paris, let's go. Just stop it." She pleads with me.

Bryce finally spoke. "No leave her here. I really need to talk to her, so we can put an end to all of this rat shit that she keeps screaming. I will drive her home Kalisha."

"Um Bryce, I'm not leaving her here, we rode together, we leave together," Kalisha stated.

"Paris! Tell your friend that I'm not going to hurt you; I just wanna talk to you."

"Okay! Kalisha I will be fine, I will call you. You can go back out there and finish talking to Jermaine." I had finally calmed down from hitting, and screaming at Bryce.

"You better not do anything to hurt her!" She hissed at him, walking out the door.

Bryce turns to me, shaking his head, breathing really hard.

"You damn women are crazy as hell!" He said walking over to the desk, grabbing his keys. "What is it that you want to talk to me about?" Trying to hurry up and get to the point.

"Let's go take a ride."

"For what? Why can't we talk right here in your office?"

"Paris, please let's just go. I don't want to talk here."

Following him out the side door of his office, praying that he would not try to kill me, or do anything stupid. The strength was not in me to fight anymore.

Chapter Seven

Bryce took the exit off of 183, pulling into Avery Ranch - another nice suburban area of Austin. I was amazed at the two-story brown brick home that we pulled up to. Stepping out of the Black Tahoe, I noticed the same smoky gray Buick Lesabre that Bryce came over in the last time.

"Who lives here?" I asked, admiring the beautiful home. He turned a key in the doorknob.

"The Boogie Man lives here, who'd you think?" he said playfully, causing a grin to stretch across my face. His crib was fly as hell. I could tell that he grew up in the Frost household; everything in his house screamed class - from the fine art on the wall, nice furniture, everything... you name it. I walked into a room that looked like a family den, with a full living room set, a pool table, and a little bar area in the far right corner.

"Would you like something to drink?" he offered, walking over to the bar and popping open a bottle of Hennessy to pour himself a drink.

"No thanks, I'm okay," I said, taking a seat. He joined me on the couch, with a brown photo album in his hand, taking a few sips of his drink. Then he began to speak, opening up the photo album.

"Okay Paris, this was my life right before I got caught up and went to prison." He showed me newspaper clippings of him shooting a layup at his basketball game, other pictures of him receiving awards, and then his high school graduation pictures with his mom. I don't recall seeing Mr. Frost or Bradley in any of the pictures, then I turned to the next page a picture of him and Bradley when they were little sitting on a boat. It looked like it was during one of their family vacations. I couldn't help but smile at the picture.

"Paris, what I need for you to understand is that I didn't have anything to do with my brother and Bradshaw getting busted. I just spent four years in prison because of the two of them; I was on my way to college with a full scholarship, headed down the right path. Until one day Bradshaw asked me to go pick up Bradley and Robert Lopez from the airport... he's my uncle, by the way - my biological father's brother. They were coming back from Miami to retrieve a package that I didn't know about. Robert was supposed to grab a couple of kilos of cocaine out of my trunk. At the airport I got pulled over, the cops found the kilos in the trunk, and just like that, my life was over... I remember it like it was yesterday, while the cops were putting me in the back of the police car, my brother - my own flesh and blood - walked by, looked at me, and kept on going without a word. Paris, if I had known that cocaine was in the trunk of that car, as God is my witness, I would have never gotten in and drove to the airport. Everything that I had worked so hard for was gone - even my girl, who I had been with since our freshman year of high school. We both got accepted into Clark University. Her parents forbid her to communicate with me, so every letter that I had written to her was returned to me. She went on off to Clark University, married a doctor and now they have a little boy together. While serving my time Bradshaw and Bradley continued to make money, they both promised me my lump sum for when I got out. After a while, the letters stopped, then the visits stopped, and then before I knew it they stopped putting money on my books. Here it is, four years later, and I still haven't gotten the money that they both promised me. So that's why I been showing up raising hell, they didn't even tell me that they moved to Westlake Hills. I went back to our old house in Anderson Mill looking for them, and they were gone. The people who now lived there gave me the address to the house in Westlake, so that's how I was able to show up at Bradshaw's birthday party. After all that happened to me I started to think about his partner from back in the day - Jamaican George, he got busted the same way I did when getting pulled over and the cops found kilos of cocaine in his trunk. That's how I know Bradshaw did that to me on purpose because he did the same thing to George."

I was speechless by the time Bryce finished telling me this heartbreaking story, I felt bad about calling him a rat and a snitch. A drink was much needed after all of that; it's crazy how everything was coming to the light about the Frost Family. Bryce held his head down after reliving everything he had gone through; my heart instantly went out to him.

"Is it okay if I fix a drink? I asked.

"Sure I'll get it for you." He got up, walked over to the bar, then came back, handing me my drink. Emotions were flowing in the air, dealing with my load of problems, and then hearing about everything that Bryce went through. Out of nowhere, I burst into tears, unable to pull myself together. I cried my eyes out uncontrollably. Bryce pulled me into his arms, holding me tight, the sound of his voice whispering into my ear sounded so sweet.

"Paris, it's going to be alright. You and the kids are going to be just fine,"

Lifting my head for air, breathing in and out, I catch a whiff of his scent. He hands me a Kleenex to wipe my eyes with, and I sit back to collect my thoughts. I catch his stare. He reaches over to wipe the last tear from my eye, pulling me in closer to him. Then he holds me in his arms, rubbing my back. "You are too beautiful to be crying," he said so softly and sweetly.

Suddenly, I wrapped my leg around Bryce's waist, straddling him. My brain went into shock as my body melted into his. This was so wrong, but it felt so damn good. His touch, his sweet kiss made me so warm and moist I couldn't stand it any longer. I knew I shouldn't, but on the other hand, I couldn't stop either; it was too late. With my body hanging halfway off the couch, Bryce began to suck on my nipples, squeezing and caressing my breasts. I quickly tore off my mini dress and threw it on the floor, but just as I was about to kick off my heels, he grabbed both of my ankles.

"No, leave those on," he breathed.

I wrapped my legs back around him. "Bryce, we shouldn't be doing this," I moaned, but he ignored me, using his teeth to pull down my black lace panties. He balled them up and pushed them in his pocket, grinning. I pulled him closer, begging him to have his way with me. "I want to feel you inside of me."

He stretched my legs wider, pulling them on top of his broad shoulders and massaging my creamy wetness. He slid his tongue down my leg, starting at my ankle and working his way to my throbbing thighs. He kissed and licked me, his tongue playing with my creamy creations, causing me to explode right onto his tongue. My body squirmed; back arched as I cried out, and my legs were shaking as if they had a mind of their own. Then Bryce flipped me over, ass all in the air, and forced himself inside of me straight doggy style. He pulled a fist full of my curls as if he was angry. If he had any frustration built up, he was definitely taking it all out on my kitty cat. I enjoyed every bit of it as he thrust himself into me; he was giving my body something that was long overdue and I didn't want this steamy episode to end. "Aw Bryce," I moaned. "Fuck me harder... Cum inside my pussy!"

Then another explosion was on its way, making me yell at the top of my lungs. As he pounded inside of me, his soft moans let me know that he was about to reach his goal. I threw my ass back at him, rubbing my dripping wet puddle all over his sack of jewels.

He grips the side of my hips extra hard and moans. "Aw Paris, I'm about to cum inside your pussy, baby!"
I grip the arm of the couch as tight as I can, urging him. "Come on, bust one!" I throw my ass back, letting him get as deep inside of me as he can. Then we climax at the same time and both of our bodies fall weak onto the couch. We drift off into a deep sleep.
The sun made its way through the blinds, the birds chirping through the windows and alarming me that morning had arrived. I managed to move my body from under Bryce as we both lay on the couch, him on top of me with his head resting on my breasts. He sits up wiping his eyes and I make my way to the bathroom.
Half an hour later, I step out of the shower; taking a good look at myself in the mirror. "Damn! What the hell have I done?" I ask myself. My mind racing 100mph, I can't believe this just happened. Questions start to run through my mind. Will he contact Bradley to inform him of what just happened? And did he do this just to get back at him from all of their previous issues? Not knowing where this mess was about to land, I was afraid of what might happen next. I finished drying myself off, putting my mini dress back on, running out to grab my purse and phone to call a cab.
"Hey, Paris. Are you hungry?" The sound of Bryce's voice appearing behind me, along with the smell of Old Spice Body Wash scent flowing through the room. Turning around to see him standing with a towel wrapped around his waist, water dripping down his chest made me want more of him. It was a must that I hurry up and get the hell out of his sight, and run far away.
"I need to call a cab so I can hurry up and get home. The kids are at your mom's house, and I need to get home so I can change clothes then go get them." Trying my best not to look at him.

" Come on Paris, you know I can take you home, why would I bring you all the way out here and let you take a cab home." He said walking closer to me, as I moved in a different direction.

"Look, Paris! Let me get dressed so I can take you home, and I promise not to bother you again."

The whole way to my house was nothing but awkwardness and silence; I couldn't even look in his direction. How was I ever going to be able to look at him or be around him with the family ever again, after him and I just performed a real life pornographic scene in his den. Low down, dirty, and shame is what I felt. How could I be so stupid?

Chapter Eight

"Baby, did you hear me? I said that my court date is next week."

I jump out of my daze, holding the phone tighter to my face. "Oh! I'm sorry sweetheart, I'm listening to you."

"What's going on with you? You're not yourself... I mean considering the fact that I'm in jail, and we don't know how much time I got. I thought you would be happy to see me, and your focus is someplace else. What's going on?"

Looking at Bradley through the glass window, my mind is all over the place. I'm unable to sit here and look my husband in the eye, because of what had taken place with his brother and I two weeks prior. Guilt is all over me, but the guilt fades away when my mind goes back to the altercation at the club with the blond-headed tramp, who later I found out her name was Tonya.

"Bradley, I need to ask you something, and I really need for you to be honest with me." I said, now looking directly at him in the eye without a blink.

He frowns with confusion written all over his face. "Ask me what Paris?"

"Is it true that you have two other kids with a woman named Tonya? I had a run-in at the club with her two weeks ago. She said that she had two kids by you."

"Hold up! What the hell are you doing at a club? Oh! So you out partying and shit when you supposed to be at home taking care of my kids?" he barked like he wanted to come through the glass window.

"*Our* kids, dammit Bradley! Don't change the subject! So is she the reason why you weren't coming home for two or three days in a row?" Trying my best not to raise my voice.

The mad as hell look on his face showed the steam and smoke coming out of his ears and nose, dents growing into his forehead.

"You little ungrateful bitch! You supposed to be holding me down and supporting me while I'm going through this shit in here, and all your little spoiled ass can do is come in here and start grilling me about something that another bitch said. Of course these hoes out here are gonna claim that they messed around with me or say they have a kid by me. What do you expect, my father is well known, and my family has money and is very well off. You just so damn young and stupid to see that these hoes wanna be you, but they can't. So you just going to let some broad out there that's bumping her gums, mess up your marriage and the lavish lifestyle that I've provided for you, over some he-say-she-say shit."

He gives me a look of disgust. I wanted so bad to jump through the glass window, grab him by his navy blue uniform, and throw him up against the wall. I was speechless and amazed at how he was turning this whole thing around on me, this dude was really incredible. Closing my eyes to breath in and out, at this point I am hotter than a Texas Firecracker.

"Bryce! Don't you dare try and put this on me, just because you don't know how to be faithful. I can't believe you have fathered two other kids outside of our marriage, you low down dirty bastard!" I barked through my clenched teeth in anger. Just as I was about to shoot out more lovely words to him, he interrupts me.

"Say let me tell you something! The next time you come here, leave whatever bullshit you done picked up out there. Next time bring my kids or let my mom bring them if you are gonna come back with some shit that I don't want to hear!"

Standing to his feet, he slammed the phone receiver down onto the hook, walking away to leave my heart sitting at the bottom of my stomach. He didn't even care that the visitation wasn't over yet; it made me feel like shit that I had pissed him off that bad to where he couldn't stand to look at me for another thirty minutes. Then again, I thought, maybe I shouldn't feel bad about Bryce.

Hours later, Kalisha was all smiles while talking about her first date with Jermaine West, sitting at the table bouncing Brielle on her lap. Placing the baked lasagna onto the dining room table next to the bread sticks, I smiled. Happy to see that my best friend was happy. We decided to do another girl's night out, but this time me cooking dinner at my house since the disaster took place at the club.

"Girl I would have never thought in a million years that Jermaine and I would be seeing each other. He is so sweet, I feel like I can talk to him about anything. Now enough about me, let's talk about you if you don't mind," she said, still bouncing Brielle on her lap, with a mischievous smirk on her face, staring directly at me.

"What about me? And why are you looking at me like that?" I playfully hissing at her.

She slid my cell phone over to me. I gave her a weird look wondering why she was giving me her phone, then she started to speak.

"It looks like our phones got mixed up again. It kept on ringing and ringing when we were at the grocery store earlier. Then I noticed the letter B kept on popping up, thinking that it was my hairdresser Brandy. When I opened the text message and read it, then that's when I realized it wasn't Brandy, and that I had accidentally grabbed your phone." She was still smirking, clicking on the message that she had already opened. My mouth dropped to the floor as I read, realizing that Kalisha had revealed my dirty little secret:

"Paris, I really do wish that you
would stop ignoring my phone calls.
What happened with us that night after
the club will stay between us, and I
put that on everything? Also, you
forgot your gold bangle after you got
out of the shower, and I would like to
return it to you. Call me!"

Closing the phone to look over at Kalisha, my mouth
was still hanging wide open. Not knowing what to say, I sat
in silence for a second until Kalisha spoke again.

"Well, me as your best friend it's my job to be nosy. So
what happened between you and Bryce, to where he is
blowing your phone up like you owe him money? Come on
girl. Spill it... I want to know!" She scooted closer to the
table, all ears and a bigger smile.

"Kalisha, I think you know what happened."

At that moment she burst into a fit. "Hell yeah I know
what happened! But I want you to tell me. Give me all the
dirty details, baby!" Cheesing away, she excitedly rocked
Brielle to sleep. But I was halfway dying inside, feeling
horrible about sleeping with my husband's brother. My
friend here on the other hand found this to be very
humorous, as she giggled her ass off.

"Look Kalisha! I did some messed up stuff, I know that
Bradley has messed around on me, but I stooped so low by
sleeping with his brother. If it was someone else then I
could accept that a little bit more, but that is still his brother
and I was wrong as hell." Trying my best not to cry, with
guilt and shame sitting inside of me.

"Okay! Paris, I do understand what you mean about
them being brothers and all, but may I remind you. This
man has fathered two other kids outside of your marriage;
he has cheated on you, has used you as a human punching
bag, and has caused you to have a miscarriage. I may be
wrong for saying this, but he deserves whatever comes his
way. He has hurt you so much Paris to the point, I had even

thought about pushing back from you for a while, because my heart couldn't take it anymore. Paris I don't want to ever see you hurt again in any kind of way." We both sat in silence until my cell phone made both of us snap out of deep thought. It was Bryce calling and I did not want to speak to him, so I let it go to voicemail. "Maybe the two of you should talk, instead of you ignoring him."

"Kalisha I don't have anything to say to him right now."

"Aw shit, Paris! We are all grown-ups here. Talk to the man, because you know he's going to keep calling until you answer the phone. It is not going to kill you if you just *talk* to him.

Just as I got ready to pour me and my motor mouth friend a glass of wine, the doorbell rings. "This better not be who I think it is." Thinking out loud and feeling frustrated, I fling open the door. Not that much surprised to see Bryce on my doorstep, dressed in all gray Armani V Neck, with black jeans and black leather jacket. Damn! This man had sexy written all over him, with his deep waves and full dark lips. No matter what, I thought to myself, I must maintain myself and keep this unwanted conversation short and simple.

"Bryce, what do you want? Why are you here?" I say, trying hard not to look at him.

"You wouldn't answer the phone, so I came over." He licked his lips with his eyes glued to me, making it very hard for me to be short and cold towards him.

Then out of nowhere Kalisha's voice appears behind me, along with the sound of her keys jingling. "Kalisha you're not leaving are you?" I give her a 'please don't go' look.

"Yes, I have to get going," she smiled. "Jermaine called, and I put Brielle to sleep in her crib."

"But it's our girls' night Kalisha!" I pouted.

"I promise to be back tomorrow, see you guys later!" She waved, skipping off.

I know damn well that Jermaine didn't call her. She wasn't slick enough to fool me. And I hated to see her go, cause Lord knows that my home girl below was gonna start talking to me the minute Bryce and I were left alone.

"Okay Bryce, what is it that you want?"

"Paris, you don't have to keep avoiding me, I'm sorry for what took place. Here, I brought your gold bangle back." Taking the bangle out of his hand, I thanked him and moved to shut the door. But Bryce stopped the door with his foot. "Look! Paris I am trying to talk to you, and you keep blowing me off," he said, following me into the house. "I haven't done anything to your bougee ass. What's your damn problem? You mad because we fucked? Well, it happened. GET OVER IT, PARIS!"

"You need to lower your damn voice in my house," I hissed. "My kids are sleeping!"

"Then why are you tripping' with me when I didn't do anything to you? Your ass played a role in that too, so be mad at your damn self."

As he turned to walk away, out of nowhere I came charging at him, hitting him with one hand and holding on to his jacket with the other. I'm not sure why I was so upset with Bryce. He was right. He hadn't done anything to harm me, and here I was attacking him like a wild woman. After allowing a few hits here and there, I guess he grew tired of it all and grabbed both of my wrists. He gripped me tight, biting his bottom lip as he jerked me back and forth.

"Let me go! Now!" I say, kicking and screaming, trying to break loose.

"Girl you better calm your crazy ass down!" he said, slamming my body up against the wall, with the same grip around both wrists. I somewhat calm down, breathing heavy like I just ran a marathon.

"Okay," I breathe heavily, finally giving up the fight.

"Are you calm now?" he said, putting his chin close to my ear, breathing onto the side of my neck.

With our bodies pushed together, our hearts racing like crazy, I feel the growth in his pants as it touches my stomach. I take in his scent, letting my eyes close as my body melts. Right there, at that moment, I wanted him inside of me; there was no way I could fight this off. After loosening his grip, I turn him around, his back now up against the wall. Dropping to my knees like I was the lady of the night, I pull his manhood out and start taking every bit of him into my mouth. I enjoy every inch of him, as I suck and slurp up and down, causing him to grip a handful of my girls. The tighter he gripped, the faster I bobbed my head up and down, gripping my lips tighter around him. He tries to control his moans, but he can't because he loves every moment of what I'm giving to him.

"Aw, Paris..." His legs start to shake, and I suck and slurp faster. He pulls himself out of my mouth, pulling me up to him by my arm.

"Baby let's go to the bedroom." he whispered into my ear.

"No, the guestroom upstairs," I replied, taking him by the hand to lead him upstairs.

Trying my best not to burst as I grind my hips back and forth on him, Bryce lies on his back, squeezing and caressing my breasts. Having him inside of me drove me crazy, I felt myself about to explode, and I couldn't hold it any longer. He felt me as my body went limp, grabbing to flip me over and put my legs on top of his shoulders. My nails sunk into his back and arms, as he grinded in and out of me. I love his aggression in the bedroom. This was how a man was supposed to handle a woman.

I blurt out as I reach my climax. "Bryce, cum inside of me!" He pumps harder and harder, exploding inside of me. Then we collapse into a puddle of exhaustion.

What the hell were we doing? Why was this happening? Why did it have to happen with his brother, and not someone else? We were both playing Russian Roulette without a care in the world. I know that if Bradley had ever gotten wind of this, he would probably have someone package us both up and be shipped off without a return address.

I wondered if that same guilt lived inside of Bradley when he went out to do his dirt. Never in a million years would I have ever thought that I would be in a situation like this. The question is, how was I going to be able to put a stop to all of this, and continue to go on like nothing ever happened? Things were already crazy enough with Bradley being gone, learning about his two other kids, and now I'm sleeping with his brother. Yeah! If I was to sell our story to a publishing company, I bet I would make millions.

After taking a long hot shower I tried to rush Bryce out before the kids woke up, but it was too late. BJ was already up watching SpongeBob in the living room.

"Hey, Uncle Bryce! I didn't know that you were here!" he said running up to the front door wearing his Spider-Man pajamas and a wide grin on his face.

"Hey Little Man! How is my nephew doing?" he said, giving BJ a hi-five.

"Uncle Bryce, can we shoot some hoops later today?"

"Yeah, if it's cool with your mom. I can come back later." Bryce replied, looking over at me with a smile on his face.

"Yeah, that's cool," I said through gritted teeth.

"Can't wait!" BJ beamed. "See you later, Uncle Bryce!" Then he skipped back to the living room to finish watching his show. Bryce stroked my hair, then offered me a quick kiss before walking out of the door.

Chapter Nine

Taking a seat next to the window at the nail salon, I think about what type of designs I wanted to get on my nails and toes. My phone interrupts my thoughts. It's Mrs. Frost's house number.

It seemed weird for her to be calling from her land line, since she always had her cell phone glued to her. I pick up, and to my surprise it was Ms. Mary calling.

"Hello?"

"Paris, you must come quickly," she whispered thickly through her Scottish accent. "Mrs. Frost has gone crazy. She's tearing up the office and the living room, throwing things everywhere!"

"Where are my kids?" I asked with urgency, rushing to get into my car. I threw my purse in the passenger seat.

"The kids and I are in the pool house. I had to remove them from the house – BJ was so scared bless his heart."

Walking straight into the house without knocking, I could hear Mrs. Frost screaming, but I can't tell from where, with the house being so big. Making my way out of the back door and running to the pool house, I made sure the kids were ok. Ms. Mary said they both had just fallen asleep, so I go back into the house trying to see what the hell was wrong with Mrs. Frost. I begin in the office, opening the door to see paper all over the place. She was sitting Indian Style in the middle of the floor, screaming and crying at the top of her lungs, her hair all over her head. She was crying so loud her voice was becoming hoarse, in a way I was kind of scared to walk over to her,

she seem to be a completely different person and I wasn't
sure what she had in mind next to throw across the room.

"Mrs. Frost... What's wrong?" I carefully take baby steps
towards her way, not knowing what to expect. I know if
Mr. Frost was here he would have come unglued, seeing all
the damage his wife has done to his office. It looked like a
tornado stopped by to pay a visit.

"I feel like God is punishing for all of my wrongs in my
life, everything is catching up with me Paris." She cries out
more, with the smell of Seagram's Gin hitting the air,
almost causing me to gag. Not sure of what the hell she was
talking about, walking over to her to take a seat on the floor
by her side, taking her hand into mines.

"Mrs. Frost, please talk to me, tell me what's going on.
Ms. Mary is scared to death to come back inside."

Her eyes were so red and swollen from all of the crying.
She begins to speak, choking on her words, picking up a
stack of papers lying next to her.

"I don't know where to begin. I just got a call saying that
Bradshaw was in the infirmary, he had a heart attack in his
cell after hearing about Bradley testifying against him. Not
only that, the doctor's found cancer and it has spread
throughout his body, and he's not doing well at all. I came
here into this office looking for life insurance policy and
some other things. Now being that I never handled any of
the bills and other financial responsibilities for this family
and household, I never knew that it was another mouth to
feed in this family. I never knew that we had another
person added on to our life insurance policy or paying for
college tuition to Florida State."

More tears come down her face as she flips through the paperwork, with me staring at her with confusion not knowing where she was going with all of this. She continues. "That husband of mine! That damned Bradshaw Frost and his sister, B, were so tight with each other, they would take each other's secrets to the grave. B never liked me and I never liked her, so that's why she never stepped foot in this house, or came to any family events. She would always go over to the real estate office and do business with Bradshaw, and never show her face. What really gets me is how much of a snake my husband is, to where he turned on Jamaican George – his best friend – the one who had his back through everything. He sets him up, putting cocaine in the trunk of his car... Jamaican George gets pulled over by the cop that's on Bradshaw's payroll, while on his way to the hospital to pick up his wife and newborn baby girl. After Jamaican George gets locked up to serve twenty five years, Bradshaw decided that wasn't enough. He wanted Jamaican George's wife Corina."

The minute she said the name Corina, she really had my full attention, all eyes and ears.

"So after he gets ol' poor George out of the way, he starts having an affair with this Corina woman. He would always tell me that she worked for him as his secretary at the office, but I knew better than that. She was young, beautiful, and high yellow. She resembled me when I was younger when Bradshaw and I first met, he would always mentioned that I was starting to age. So that's what caused me to have all of this work done to my face and body, but no matter how much work I had done to myself, it still didn't keep him away from Corina – he was in love with her and he was planning to leave me for her. I didn't know what I was going to do financially if Bradshaw decided to throw me and Bradley out for this woman, so I hooked up with Johnny Lopez; one of Bradshaw's associates. He healed my wounds, he loved me, gave me everything I wanted. Our secret affair went on for years and years. Bradshaw wouldn't be home for weeks sometimes, so that left plenty of time for me to be with Johnny. In the mix of all of that, I got pregnant with Bryce. As soon as I found out that I was pregnant, Johnny wanted us to move away to Hawaii, so we could be a happy family together. The day I made it home to pack up me and Bradly's things, to my surprise Bradshaw was sitting in the living room, waiting on me, with a red gift wrapped box in his lap, wearing a smile on his face."

Mrs. Frost touch a hand to her cheek, deep in reminiscence. 'Hey Honey, I miss you,' he said. And I said, 'Bradshaw, I'm leaving you. I want a divorce.' He gets up, walking over to me, and hands me the gift box, still smiling. Then he says, 'Ok sweetheart, I have something to give you before you walk out of my life.' And after placing young Bradley on the couch, nervous and scared, I realize Bradshaw was being too calm for a situation like this. Lifting open the top part of the gift box, I see what seems to look like a mannequin's head from a Cosmetology School, covered in plastic. The minute I remove the plastic from inside the box, I begin to scream. I scream so loud, Bradley woke up, so afraid he grabbed his daddy by leg. Bradshaw didn't budge one bit. He just stood there with that same wicked smile on his face, as I dropped the box to the floor with Johnny's frozen head rolling out going under the coffee table. My heart sunk so low into the bottom of my stomach, my body fell so weak to the floor. After that day I haven't been myself completely, Bradshaw just don't know when he killed Johnny, a part of me died to. I still hurt right now today, not even my revenge was able to heal my heart. I felt like Bradshaw should hurt just as bad as I hurt when he took Johnny away from me, so years later on down the road I had someone to locate this precious Corina of his, just to find out he put her up in a house located in Pflugerville owned by his sister B. After learning Corina's day to day routine, I hired someone to send her on a very long permanent vacation with no return. He killed my Johnny, so I had his Corina wiped off the planet. However a part of Corina is still running around here on earth that I wasn't aware of until now, coming across these photos and tuition payment receipts to Florida State University."

Just as she placed the photos into my hand, my eyes are in shock. My mind is completely screwed up, this can't be, and this world cannot be this small. My heart is about to jump out of my chest, my eyes are super glued to the pictures. The first picture of my beautiful mother wearing red spaghetti strap mini dress, sitting on Mr. Frost's lap smiling like a happy couple. Judging from the background of the picture it looked like they were in Las Vegas or Atlantic City. The second one – a graduation picture of my baby sister who had grown into a beautiful young lady, dressed in her blue and white cap and gown. Smiling as she's holding up her high school diploma, standing in the middle of Mr. Frost and that heifer, Betty, who turned my world upside down the day she came and took my sister from me. Along with the photos was a stack of my mother's obituaries, and other photos taken during her funeral with her laying in her coffin surrounded by giant floral arrangements.

Breathing becomes difficult; it feels like someone is squeezing me around the middle and the palms of my hands begin to sweat. My stomach is tied in a knot and I forget that Mrs. Frost is right in front of me, crying about her news, when her words replay in my mind, *I hired someone to send her on a very long permanent vacation with no return.*

Looking back at the pictures of my mother, and then at Mrs. Frost, rage took over me as my hands gripped around her long pencil neck. I try my best to choke every ounce of silicone and Botox out of her, and she did her best to fight for her life.

"YOU BITCH! YOU KILLED MY MOTHER!" I screamed so loud into her ear as I continued to choke her, jerking her neck back and forth as the back of her head banged against the hard wooden floor. Her legs and arms flapped like a fish out of water. She reached for something, but I couldn't tell what it is because I'm trying my best to choke the life out of her. Out of nowhere Mrs. Frost gives me a painful whack to the right side of my head with the lamp, breaking the light bulb that she managed to pull off the table by the cord, causing me to roll over by the desk with blood coming from my head. Taking the blow to my head doesn't stop me at all. Jumping up to notice Mrs. Frost crawling towards the door, trying to catch her breath, I immediately fly into her direction. Taking both fist full of her tangled wet-and-wavy do, dragging her out of the office through the living room as she grabs the leg of every piece of furniture she can, turning over chairs and tables. Every time she managed to grab anything, I would stomp it right out of her hand.

"SOMEBODY HELP ME! HELP!" she yelled, trying to scream as loud as she could, but her voice had already gone hoarse from her constant cries earlier. Making my way out of the back door that lead to the swimming pool, still with a fist full of her hair, as she was still kicking and screaming. The minute I got her body close to the edge of the pool, she just didn't know that it was more kicking and flapping she was about to do. I made it a point to not let her ass come up for no air at all, making sure that I applied all of my weight pressure with both hands holding her head under water. At this moment I am a completely different person to where I'm starting to scare my damn self; the only thing that sticks to my brain is that she killed my mother. She took away the most precious thing in my life, the woman who carried me for nine months. As I continued holding her head under water, I was making it a point to end her life right there in her own backyard, not giving a damn about anything at that moment. That is until I looked up; hearing the sound of my son's screaming voice.

"Mommy, Mommy! Don't hurt Grandma! Mommy stop it!" BJ was standing in the doorway of the pool house, crying his little heart out. Ms. Mary standing right behind him with Brielle in her arms holding the cordless phone up to her ear. They must have been watching for a good while because the minute I let Mrs. Frost head go, she comes up for air coughing and spitting up water. As soon as I started walking in the direction of my kids, I'm stopped right in my track not taking another step.

"FREEZE! GET ON THE GROUND! PUT YOUR HANDS BEHINE YOUR HEAD! "

Barley turning my head to look behind me, I knew that Westlake Police meant business. Seeing how their guns were drawn on me, I knew that I had better get my ass on the ground and do what I was told. Being handcuffed and hauled off into the police car, hearing my kids' cries were the only thing that made me break and regret my actions.

Two days after being booked and finger printed with a jacked up mugshot, and given an ugly light blue jail uniform, chills went up my spine when hearing the metal door slam shut. All alone in a dark six by eight cell, a filthy toilet and sink within arm reach, sitting on a mattress that was flat as a pancake. The scariest thing about arriving to jail for the first time of your life, is not knowing what's going to happen or how long you were going to be in there. I already knew right off the back my charges were aggravated assault and attempted murder was on my hands. Never been to law school before a day in my life, but one thing I do know, is that for some reason old backwards ass Texas will give you more time for attempted murder verses actual murder. Either way it goes, My life was up shit creek and there was no telling when I was getting out. Now my kids will have to grow up with both parents behind bars, just perfect. Right about now, I just want to drift off into a deep sleep and never wake up again. My life of five years has been a complete nightmare, I'm surprise that I haven't ended up in a mental institution, or strung out on drugs.

The sound of keys unlocking the metal door causes me to jump, scaring the hell out of me with the tall, slender

NBA basketball player looking black female guard standing there.

"Hey, Frost!" she shouts out my last name that I regret taking it after exchanging vowels.

"The nurse wants to see you!" she shouted as if I was deaf.

"What the nurse wanna see me for?" I asked, confused.

"Get up and let's go find out."

Walking over to her, I wondering why in the hell she was placing cuffs onto my wrist, when I was already in jail, where in the hell was I going to run off to. We entered the nurse's station and I sat in a white plastic chair, still cuffed in the front.

"After you finish up here with the nurse, someone is here to see you," she said before walking out of the door. The stubby old nurse, who looked like she was about ready for retirement, came walking in with paperwork in her hand.

"Paris Frost?" she said. "I'm Ms. Tucker. I requested for you to come back to see me for your urine and blood test results. They both show that you are pregnant."

I stare at her like she has lost her mind, as she stands in front of me handing me my medical paperwork. We need to get you started on prenatal vitamins right away, and start weekly checkups."

I know damn well this woman did not just tell me that I'm pregnant. I silently kicked myself, knowing good and well I shouldn't have been shocked. After all, I knew I was playing a dangerous game with Bryce. Nonetheless, I was stuck trying to digest another set of news. Then the guard came back in just as the nurse left out.

"Come on Frost, someone is here to see you."

Everything was too overwhelming, too much was happening. I was just ready to go back to my cell and lay there, hoping that I wouldn't wake back up. Whoever was here to see me, they were about to get cursed out if they were bringing in any other bad news.

I was shocked to see Marshall Duncan, Bradley's lawyer sitting at the glass window, wearing an all-white suit and a white cowboy hat.

"Mr. Duncan, what are you doing here?" I asked placing the phone receiver up to my ear. "Hello Paris, Bryce contacted me told me what happened, so I came out do what I can. In a few hours, you'll be free to go home. "

"Are you sure Mr. Duncan?" I asked confused, but relieved at the same time.

"Yes, they re-opened the investigation on your mother's death on account of what you reported to the police about Gloria's confession. When questioning Mrs. Frost about the incident at her house, she confessed about everything. So now she's in custody, and you are free. Your record will be fine, so that's another thing that you don't have to worry about." After tilting his cowboy hat he walked away, and within an hour and a half I was walking out as a free woman. My girl Kalisha waiting for me out front being by my side like always. As much drama I kept in my life, I'm surprise that Kalisha hadn't disowned me.

Drying off from the long hot shower to relax my nerves, with a belly full of take-out from Red Lobster that Kalisha and I had, words could not explain how happy I was to be home with my kids, two days without them felt like two years. My first night home, I let both of them sleep in the bed with me, I missed my babies so much. Lying in bed watching my two angels sleep reminded me that I needed to make a doctor's appointment, and locate an abortion clinic. There was no way that I could bring a child into this world at this moment with everything going on, learning about my mother's death, along with Mr. Frost being London's biological father was weighing pounds onto my heart. With all of the stress I did not want to suffer from another miscarriage, not only that, but the seed that I was now carrying did not belong to my husband. It belonged to his brother and that was just not something that I wanted to deal with, there were already enough secrets, lies, and all types of skeletons locked in this family's closet, or buried some place. The cycle was to be stopped right here and right now.

Chapter Ten

The two and a half hour drive to Huntsville was a challenge with the kids, and it didn't help constantly having to pull over because of my morning sickness.

"Mommy is your tummy upset? Did you bring the pink stuff so your tummy can feel better?" My sweet BJ asked with concern, as he snacked on his apple cereal bar in the back seat with Brielle as she was falling asleep.

"Yes, baby! Mommy will be just fine." I replied back after gargling my travel size mouth wash, stepping back into the car, looking into my rear view mirror.

Entering the front office to check in with the officers and completing the pat down search, the kids and I take a seat in the far left back corner of the visitation room.

"Mommy, is daddy coming home with us today?" BJ asked with the sweetest look on his face, looking just like his father.

"No, baby. Daddy has to stay here for a while. We can't take him home, but we can come visit him on weekends," I explain to him, rubbing the top of his fresh low cut fade.

It hurt me to see sadness in my kids' eyes; I really wish that things could be different for them. They deserved so much more than having to visit their father in prison.

My heart somewhat melted when Bradley walked out, wearing all white prison uniform walking over to our table. His weight picked up in all of the right places, I could tell that he been hitting the weights daily. Through all the hell and back, he still looked so damn sexy, but just because he looked good doesn't mean that he was good for me.

"Hey! What's up my Queen?" We exchanged hugs as I passed Brielle off to him, then let BJ give him a hug and hi-five. To my surprise Brielle sat calm with him, considering it was coming close to a whole year since Bradley had been gone.

"Paris, thank you so much for bringing the kids to see me. I really needed that, you just don't know how happy I am to see all of you." He stares at me, noticing my distant demeanor.

"I will do the best I can Bradley with bringing the kids on weekends, but I really need to seek help with everything that has taken place, mentally it has messed me up big time."

"Paris. I want to say again that I am sorry for everything that I have done, and I am sorry for what my family has done. I had no idea that my father and your mom had something going on and conceived a child with each other, and as far as my Auntie B, she was so damn private with her life. The only time I got see her was when she would come to the office to do business with my dad, and now she's locked up right along with us. I had no clue that she was raising one of his outside kids."

"How long are you going to be in here?" I asked not wanting to get into the disturbed conversation in front of BJ, who could fully understand everything that was going on. It was bad enough that he had to witness me holding his Grandmother's head under water, then been hauled off to jail. My kids had really had enough.

"Well, they gave me fifteen years. I know that I did the most rotten shit to my father by ratting on him, but he also did some messed up stuff. I'm not about to get into all of that. What's done is done. I can't take it back." He placed Brielle over his shoulder, rubbing her back. It really amazes me how he could do something so cold, and not show a once of regret or sympathy. Like the saying goes – The apple don't fall too far from the tree.

"I know you might not care to talk about this," he said hesitantly. "But do you know how much time they gave my mom for what she did?"

"She only got twenty five years for what she had done to my mother; I wish they would have given her the electric chair." I hissed at him, wanting him to feel where I was coming from. During the rest of the visit, I didn't say much. I just let him have his time with the kids, until the two hours was up.

"Hey Paris, I need you to do me a favor," he said tapping my hand from across the table.

"What is it Bradley?" I said, feeling annoyed.

"Look, I need for you to get a mini storage unit, take the black leather furniture set that's in the garage, get the two giant teddy bears that I bought for the kids, and put it into storage for me please."

"Why?"

"Because I said so Paris," he hissed. "Now, please, just do that for me."

"Ok, whatever you say Dear," I said, giving him a fake smile. And I was happy that the guard came over to inform us that visitation was over. My stomach was turning, and I really needed to go to the bathroom. This was the worst pregnancy ever; I didn't only get morning sickness. I had noon sickness and night sickness.

"Oh, before we go! Bradley where is your father? " I asked taking Brielle out of his arms.

"He is in Galveston at the prison hospital, he really not doing good at all."

"Ok, I will bring the kids back next weekend."

Walking out on a mission to get closer, it was a must that I made it to Galveston to pay Mr. Frost a visit before he left this earth.

The following weekend rolled around fast just like I wanted, I let Bryce take BJ to visit Bradley for that weekend, and left Brielle with Kalisha. Then I proceeded off to Galveston, to pay this old shriveled up vegetable a visit. Walking into the infirmary with different hospital inmates laying up all wounded or just dying, it was kind of sad to see the inmates dying while being incarcerated and not being able to pass away in their home with family around them. Approaching Mr. Frost's bedside he didn't look like himself at all. He had lost all of his hair and weight; teeth were missing and his nails long and dark looking. The minute he saw me walk in, he pressed the button for his bed to rise up, surprised to see me.

"Paris, what brings you by to see me?" He spoke in a raspy voice, he sounded like it was painful for him to talk. I didn't give a shit about how much pain he was in.

"Question marks are what bring me here today Mr. Frost," I replied, pulling up a chair next to his bed, but not too close. I didn't want to give him the idea that we were about to have no heart to heart, father and daughter in-law conversation.

"Mr. Frost, I know about you and my mom, and I also know that you are the father of my little sister, London. You knew all this time while Bradley and I were together. I wracked my brain back and forth, trying to figure out for the life of me, why you had such a strong dislike towards me since day one when I hadn't done anything to you but show you respect the whole time. Instead of you being a man by confessing your wrongs, you do everything in your power to tear Bradley and me apart because you were so afraid of your skeletons falling out of the closet. You just don't know that you have been making my life a living hell way before I had even met your son and you knew who I was the whole damn time. All I want to know is how can I get in contact with my sister, if you could please give me London's contact information before taking your last breath I would gladly appreciate that."

He struggles to reach for his pitcher of water to take a sip; I don't bother to help him at all. "Paris, I don't know where to begin. I will do my best to tell you everything you want to know. That's the least I can do. The day I laid eyes on your mother that was the day I fell in love with her. There was only one problem. She was my best friend's wife, and he loved her so much. George and I had started hustling together when he arrived from Kingston, Jamaica our last year of high school. That's how he got the name, Jamaican George, and we had been the best of friends ever since. He loved your mother and she loved him. They got married in New Orleans and a little after your mom became pregnant with you. That's when George wanted to get out of the game, and open up a legit business because he was about to be a father. He had what I wanted, which was your mother and happiness. Even though I was married to Gloria and we had Bradley, I still wasn't happy. George was a well-educated guy, he had street smarts and book smarts, so of course he made way more money than I did. I envied him so much; I wanted him out of the way. So the day your mom was supposed to leave the hospital to go home from giving birth to you, I had him set up and pulled over by the cops. Your mother didn't have anyone but him, so when he didn't arrive to take the two of you home from the hospital, she called me. Ever since that day I have been in her life. I got my sister to purchase a house in Pflugerville and moved you and your mom into the house so George wouldn't have any type of contact with her if he tried to call or write. I wanted her to believe that he abandoned the two of you, just so I can have her all to myself. Your mother would never bring me around you or allow me to come to the house, she never wanted to set the wrong example for you and London, having a man coming and going in and out of the house. The day London was born your mother hurt me so bad by not giving her the last name, instead she gave her George's last name – Scott. She still carried on his last name. After fourteen years of being with your mom, I went home to tell Gloria that I was leaving her. That's when one of my associates called to tell me that Corina died of a drug overdose, and my heart hasn't been right ever since that day. I guess that was the revenge for me killing Johnny Lopez. If I could turn back time, I would have sat my pride to the side and let Gloria go off to be with Johnny, and I could have went on to be with your mother."

He takes another sip of his water, coughing and breathing hard. I sit looking at him with disgust. Standing to my feet, walking closer to him, I try my best to keep my hands to myself.

"You know it is taking everything in me to not pull out all of these cords and tubes that you are hooked up to, and wrap them around your neck until your eyeballs pop out of your head," I said, my voice quivering. "However, I got two kids at home that need me, so I will let God deal with you on that note. From the looks of your condition, you might be suffering just enough. Now give me London's contact information, so I can get out of this stink hole."

With a pen one of the nurses let me have, I jotted her number down as he gave it to me. Then I stare at his pitiful form as he looks at me with sadness in his eyes, but that didn't move me one bit. "Thanks for the number. May God have mercy on your soul."

Then I storm out of the room in silent tears, jumping into the black Tahoe and preparing to make my way through Houston's traffic. This was unbelievable; my head was officially screwed up. There was no way I could function in this bumper to bumper traffic. So I took the next exit, pulling into the parking lot of Timmy Chan's, and taking a couple of deep breaths before dialing my sister's number. Hearing the sound of her voice was a breath of fresh air, tears were nonstop. We chatted for so long before I knew it the sun was going down, and my phone was about to die.

"London! I'm going to fly you here to Austin, just let me know when you have a break from school. I don't want to interrupt your studies." I said still crying.

"Ok, sis. I'll let you know!" she said in a cheerful voice.

"One more thing, London, please know that I never stopped loving you. I always wondered where you were, and what you were doing. I love you."

"I love you too, Paris. I'll see you soon."

Listening to the sound of the sonogram machine and the baby's heartbeat as I lie on top of the exam table, the doctor moved the monitor back and forth across my stomach.

"Well, Paris, it looks like we have two heartbeats here," the nurse said, wiping the jelly off my stomach. "With you being as far along as you are, it's really dangerous for you to try and have the pregnancy terminated. You might want to consider other options."

I shot straight up. "What do you mean, two heartbeats?"

"You are three and a half months pregnant with twins Paris."

After collecting my paperwork and leaving to go home, I dial Bryce's number as I approach the red light.

"Hey, Paris!"

"I really need to talk to you, can you come over tonight?"

"Yeah, I just have to work on some stuff here at the club; I'll be over when I'm done."

"Cool," I said. And I barely remembered hanging up.

Since the kids fell asleep in the living room, I decided to go clean up there room. Putting all of the toys and books away, I almost forgot that I had asked Bryce to come over when the knock at the door startled me.

"Hey! How are you doing? " I said, answering the door. He was wearing a white t-shirt, starched blue jeans, and a pair of black Chuck Taylor's. Just as sexy as he could be. I try not to stare too hard at him, because tonight was not the night.

"I'm good. Is everything ok?"

"Yeah, I'm up in the kids' room, cleaning."

Bryce follows me back up to their room and leans up against the wall with his arms folded. "Bryce, I don't know how you are going to take this, but when I was in jail I found out that I was pregnant, and today the doctor just told me that I'm close to four months, carrying twins." I paused for a minute to see his reaction, but he only continues to stand there with his arms folded. I'm feeling a bit nervous without a right away response from him, staring at me with a straight face. Frustration over comes me, slamming the dresser drawer shut making an attempt to storm out of the room.

"Forget it then! I don't even know why I bothered! You can just leave! " I yelled out to him, walking out of the door. Then he took me by the hand to pull me closer to him, I try pull away.

"Paris! Would you calm down? It's taking me a minute to digest this, damn!" Still pulling me closer to him, he places his hand onto my stomach with his other hand around my waist, speaking in a calm volume not taking his eyes off of me. "How do you feel? What do you want to do?"

"Well, considering the circumstances my plan was to have an abortion, but the doctor said that it could be dangerous with me being close to four months. Bryce I don't know if I can do this. " I'm trying my best not to cry, but can't hold the tears any longer.

"You don't know if you can do what Paris?" He raised his voice, turning me loose with anger.

"I can't have a baby by you, Bryce," I hissed. "I am married to your brother, for crying out loud! Don't you think this situation with us is already disturbing, and not to mention everything that just came to the light about what your family did to my family? I'm already worried about my kids becoming dysfunctional, I don't want them growing up being double related to siblings who are also their cousins. Your family already has enough screwed up genes; why in the hell would I want to reproduce with another Frost?" Catching the last few words of what I just blurted out, I noticed rage and anger written all over Bryce's face.

"FUCK YOU, BITCH!" The words cut like a knife. Standing there in shock, the fact that Bryce would speak to me that way hurt me to the core, and I couldn't do anything but stare at him with tears in my eyes.

"Paris, I am so sorry."

"No! Leave me alone! GET OUT!" I screamed just as he tried to grab me, I picked up the pink giant teddy bear sitting next to Brielle's crib, swinging it at him as he jumped out of the way, the blade to the spinning ceiling fan caught the teddy bear by the head. Cotton mixed with bundles of one hundred dollar bills came falling out of nowhere, Bryce and I standing in the middle of the kids room. Our mouths wide open, feet glued to the floor.

"What the hell?" We both shouted at the same time.

Something that Bradley told me during the visit came back to my mind, when he stated that he wanted me to put the black leather living room set in storage, along with two giant teddy bears. I walked over to grab the blue teddy bear, trying to rip the head off with my bear hands. Bryce took it out of my hand, whipping out his pocket knife.

"Watch out, let me see something." Flipping the bear over to slit the back of it carefully, he stuck his hand inside to pull out more cotton mixed in with bundles of one hundred dollar bills. After Bryce and I pulled another stash out from the cushions of the living room couches in the garage, and two days of counting everything on the money counting machine. I could not believe that Bradley had over half of a million dollars hidden in the house, and didn't even bother to tell me, not giving a damn about how me and his two kids were gonna live. His plan was to just serve his time, and then come home to his stacks of Franklins. Well he was gonna be in for a big surprise.

Chapter Eleven

Arriving to Austin Bergstrom Airport with all smiles, I was feeling anxious and happy all rolled up in one. The summer of 2006 had arrived, and so did my baby sister, two weeks after the birth of my twins, Braylon and Brianna. I spotted her, still just as petite as ever with her girlish, hourglass frame. I jumped out of the car almost forgetting to put it in park, and rushed to meet her. She wore a pair of purple shorts and a half t-shirt, showing off her pierced belly button, and blond highlights ripped through her hair. She noticed me, too, and ran to meet me. We embraced each other for a good minute along with a river of tears; I even notice that she still wore the gold bangle on her wrist that I gave her the day she was taken away. Being caught up in the moment I forgot that the parking was only for a couple of minutes, until the security guard tapped me on my shoulder.

"Ma'am I'm sorry, but we need you to load your bags into the car to make room for others to pick up." He was very polite.

After apologizing and loading London's bags into the car, we proceeded to hit the road. London instantly fell in love with all four of her nieces and nephews, as BJ and Brielle both crawled into her lap at the same time.

Back at home, we sat at the dinner table having a nice welcome home BB-Q dinner that Bryce hooked up on the new grill in the backyard.

"BJ and Brielle! Please let Auntie London enjoy her meal, she just got here." I fussed while burping Braylon over my shoulder, and Bryce rocking Brianna to sleep.

"Aw sis, it's cool, they're just happy to see their auntie, that's all!" She playfully kissed them both on the forehead, then she turned to me with a huge smile.

"Paris you have a beautiful home, you are very blessed."

Bryce and I glare at each other as we both rocked the babies.

"Thank you my love. After the kids go to sleep why don't you and I go for a drive?" I suggested with a smile.

Parking right in front of the old house that used to be our home in Pflugerville, London turns to me with sadness in her eyes.

"I wonder who lives here now," she said, looking out of the window.

"I'm not sure... I wonder the same thing."

"Paris, she promised me that she would bring me back to see you," London said suddenly. "I even wrote you letters, but you never responded. She told me that you didn't want to see me anymore and that you went on and moved out of state. Then she would tell me that mom was a junkie whore, and you were going to follow right in her footsteps." My sister burst into tears, and it hurt me that she spent all these years thinking that I didn't want to have anything to do with her. It made me damn near wish death on Betty and Mr. Frost. There was no need to do that, though, because they both were already suffering, being locked up in prison.

"London, that is not true about mom or me. I will tell you everything that I just found out, but know this – I never changed my cell number, just in case you ever called. I was kicked out of this house the day after she came and took you away, so that's why I never got any of your letters."

Once I gave London the full story about the history and foundation that tore us apart, she was in shock to learn the truth. She sat quietly the whole time on our way back to the house, wiping away a few tear drops here and there. Walking into the house, we noticed Bryce coming in through the back sliding door from the backyard, Bryce walks up to me taking my hand into his. "Paris you have a visitor in the backyard, come with me."

He took my hand, leading me out onto the back porch. My eyes scanned the grass area thinking that he had gotten me a puppy, but my focus is directed to my left. Somebody had called my name with a thick accent. It was a tall man, with shoulder length dreadlocks. Looking into his eyes observing his facial features, I saw an older version of my son BJ. Even though BJ did look like Bradley, but he still carried other strong features. He steps closer to me, and I can't take my eyes off of him.

"Paris... I am your father – George Scott. "

I'm puzzled; I stand there studying all of him, taking in his words. He wipes the tear from my right eye; I can't believe this is the other part of me standing right before my eyes.

"Come to me, my daughter." He speaks again, taking me into his arms, and I break down.

"Don't worry baby girl, Daddy is here now." He held me in his arms so tight, as if he never wanted to let go.

Two years later after selling the house, cars, and other rental property that Bradley had. I filed for a divorce; Bryce sold his house and his club. We both took the kids to start a new life in Houston, in a big beautiful two story house. My father purchased a home around the corner from us and opened up a limo service. After Mr. Frost's passing, London was given the house in Westlake Hills and received all of the money that was left over in the bank accounts. She sold the house, transferred to Houston and moved into a nice size one story home in Houston's Clear Lake area. I was attending Nursing School for my Master's - something that I always dreamed about doing, and I was grateful that I could go to school full time not having to work.

Kalisha and Jermaine got married in the Bahamas and were expecting a baby girl; she asked if it was ok if they named her Corina. My mother's name, of course my response was yes. However Bradley was never informed about my pregnancy of the twins by his brother. When my pregnancy was starting to show I stopped taking the kids to visit him, shortly after that the letters stopped. Bryce would always send money on his books, and he would send him pictures of the kids, but of course me or the twins were nowhere in the photos. Bryce went into his own Prime Real Estate Business and he opened a nice upscale club in Houston. Both his real estate business and club was doing very well to where he didn't have to deal any type of drugs or any illegal activities at all. He was able to take care of all of us from what his businesses brought in, and not to mention my humongous stash that rested in my account that I never had to touch. That was my conformation to say I was good with or without Bryce. One beautiful sunny afternoon my father pulled me to the side while he was out back doing some yard work with Bryce. Not sure what he wanted to talk about, so I laid the twins down for their nap and took a walk with my father in our beautiful upscale neighborhood, passing by the other giant homes as the Nannies and Housekeepers strolled through walking the family dogs, and pushing the kids in the strollers. "So, what's up dad? What did you want to talk about that was so important to where you pulled my out of the AC at home, and you know I can't stand the heat."

I playfully whined at him as I poked my bottom lip out.

"Aw, Honey, it's not that bad." He smiled, taking my hand.

"Honey, I know it's been a huge adjustment these past couple of years with me being in your life for the first time ever, it stills bothers me that I have missed out on 23 years of your life, but the only thing I can do is continue to make the best of it, and enjoy every bit of time with you and my grandchildren."

I look up to smile at him, but my smile fade away when I notice sadness in his eyes.

"Daddy, what's on your mind?" I asked worried.

"Paris, I want to share something with you sweetie. I hope and pray that you don't see me any different, I hope that you still look at me as your father like you always have since the day I walked into your life two years ago. " He took a deep breath.

"Daddy, just spit it out." I told him as I rubbed his back.

"Well, you know I was locked up in Galveston area, the same place where Bradshaw was located at in the infirmary. One of our old running buddies by the name of

Carl was working as a janitor in the infirmary. He was housed in a couple of cells down from me. Anyway he came to inform me that Bradshaw was located there damn near on his death bed, and was about to croak over at any moment. I had two weeks left before my release date, the first thing on my agenda was to go looking for Bradshaw as soon as I got out, but since it was no need for me to go and do that, with him being so close. I decided to fill in for Carl when he purposely shut his own foot in the door, causing swelling so he could have a reason to not report to work. Strolling along in the hall way with my mop, taking notice to the open door that read Frost on a white sign at the foot of the hospital bed. I quietly mopped my way in right up to his bed, as his weak looking body laid there sleeping in peace. He must have felt someone standing over him, causing him to wake up. Blinking his eyes for a double take, the minute we made eye contact, the first word to shoot out of my mouth was "why?"

Once catching his vision to realize that he wasn't dreaming, or having a nightmare. He manages to say my name "George" in a hoarse raspy voice. Fear was written all over him. I nodded to let him know that it was me, the same buddy that he had set up and sent to prison, only to take off with his wife.

Once he made the attempt to reach for his water sitting on top of the hospital over bed table, I use my foot to push the table back away from him, causing him not being able to reach for his water. He looks at me with sadness in his eyes. The only thing I could think of was my beautiful wife Corina and you Paris. How he had me set up to get pulled over in the hospital parking lot when I was coming to take you and your mother home. He was real low down and dirty. Paris I wouldn't wish nothing like that on my worst enemy, for you to do something like that to someone, you'd have got have an icicle for a heart.

Out of nowhere my hands were wrapped around his little frail neck. Squeezing as tight as I could. I looked him dead in his eyes without a blink, as he struggled to fight for air, trying to pull my fingers apart from around his neck, but his body being so weak he doesn't succeed at all. After laying him to rest; I mop my way back out to finish up the rest of my duties, grabbed a bag of Lays Potato Chips from my locker, and laid down in my bunk to snack and read a Jet Magazine like nothing had ever happen. Two weeks later I was released, walking out of that damn slave system, without a regretful bone in my body for what I did to that snake bastard."

After my father revealed everything to me, it seemed like pounds were lifted off of his shoulders by the time we circled back around to the house. I was a little in shock that my father was the one who took Mr. Frost life away, but however at the same time I was not surprised at all. The only thing I could think of was too bad I couldn't send Mrs. Frost to hell right along with her snake husband, since she was the one responsible for my mother's death. But I would have to take what I could get. The most important thing was that I had my family, and we were living well. Thank you, Frost family.

New Life

New Beginnings

New Frost Family

New Situations

Chapter Twelve

Paris put her silver BMW in park of the drive way of her beautiful River Oaks home. She and her family had been here for nine whole years since relocating to Houston. Her mind drifts back to the lunch date she'd just had with her sister. She noticed London was acting a little weird after she had asked her about when was she going to settled down with a husband and kids. But she disregarded the thought when B.J came outside to the porch, his basketball in hand.

He was ready to go do what he did best, which was shoot some hoops with his friends. She couldn't believe how tall he had gotten, and how he was growing to be a very handsome young man. She stepped out of the car, wearing a purple sleeveless jumpsuit. She wore matching purple heels, and her Spanish waves hung down the middle of her back. B.J approached his mother, still dribbling his basketball.

"Hey, mom! Do you have any bags that you want me to take in the house for you?"

Paris shuts the car door, turns around and responds. Her smile fades away as she takes a couple of steps back, leaning up against the car. She is now waring a blank stare on her face, as if she just had seen a ghost.

"Mom, what's wrong? Are you okay?" B.J asks with concern, walking closer to his mother, with his hand extended out.

"Um, yes baby. I'm fine. I don't have any bags in the car, today I only went out to lunch with your Auntie London and that was it. You mean to tell me that you are going to go play basketball out in this heat?" she asked referring to the August weather, and trying to wipe off the weird look on her face, hoping that B.J didn't notice the way she was looking at him.

"No mom. Justin, Ayden, and I were going over to the indoor gym." He replied back, still with a concern look on his face.

"Well, okay sweetie. Just be careful" She said still being somewhat distant towards her son.

"Mom! Are you sure that you are okay?" B.J asked again noticing that something wasn't right with his mother.

"Yes Honey. I just need to go lay down. Your Auntie London had me all over Houston today." She said forcing herself to laugh.

"Well, Okay Mom. I'll be back, I love you." He said, placing a kiss on her left cheek, before taking off.

Paris must have forgotten how advanced and intelligent B.J was for his age. He was far from stupid; he was the type of kid that you could not just tell him anything. Even though Paris thinks that her son don't notice everything, but he do. He even notices how lately she hasn't been able to look at him in the eye for too long, or how she tries to avoid him sometimes. Although she still gives him that mothers love, but she gives it to him with some type of distance. The guilt and emotions that sat at the pit of her stomach, was the reason for Paris's odd behavior towards her son. No matter how much she tried to erase her ex-husband out of her head, she could not do it. Due to the fact that she saw him every single day when she look at her son, B.J. He was the spitting image of his father from head to toe; he carried such strong features that brought back so many painful memories that were eating at her emotions. The guilt that sat in the pit of her stomach comes from the fact that she birthed a set of twins from his brother.

Paris strutted her way into the family room. She noticed Brielle sleeping in the Lazy Boy with Pebbles, the family's Miniature Yorkie. The now nine-year-old twins, Braylon and Brianna, were knocked out on the couch, one of them at each end. She always loved to watch her kids as they slept in peace, ever since the day they were born.

She quickly made her way to the master bedroom, locking the door behind her. She inhales the combination smell of body soap, and Dolce and Gabbana Men Fragrance. That let her know that Bryce had just stepped out of the shower, and she wanted him right then and there. Especially while the kids were taking their afternoon nap, and with B.J gone out to play basketball.

"Sweetie! I'm home," Paris said through the closed bathroom door.

Bryce opened the door, with a royal blue towel wrapped around his waist. His broad chest exposed. Paris couldn't help herself, not able to keep her hands off of him. After nine years of being with him, she was still very attracted to him. With his honey brown complexion, and full dark grape colored lips.

"Hey baby, did you enjoy your lunch date?" he asked placing a kiss on her lips, admiring how beautiful she always looked.

"Yes I did. Now I'm ready for dessert." she said stepping closer to him, making direct eye contact. Biting her bottom lip, as she snatched the towel from around his waist;

dropping to her knees, taking in all of him into her mouth. Sucking and slurping every inch of him. Bryce leans his head back against the bathroom door, his eyes closed tight, enjoying the moment. She nibbled the tip of him, still sucking him nice and slow. It really turned him on how Paris handled him in the bedroom, she was a freak and he loved every bit of it. She was really never able to be herself in the bedroom with Bradley. He was either always gone for days or weeks at a time. Then during the very few moments he was intimate with her, he would do his thing not bothering to make sure she was satisfied. Now on the other hand with Bryce, he allowed her to do just about anything she wanted. Plus he made sure that she was always satisfied.

Dropping her jumper and lace panties to the floor, leaving her heels on, she struts over to the king sized bed, with her seductive moves. Lying across the bed, spreading her legs apart wide open. To where both legs nearly reaches the back of her head. Bryce now stands before her, admiring her pink wetness. She always turned him on whenever she walked around the bedroom naked with heels on. Even after birthing four kids, her body was still amazing.

Her back starts to arch right along with her moans, just as Bryce slides his long warm tongue in and out of her wetness. She begs him for more, as both of her legs wraps around his head, and his neck. He continues to please her by sucking, and licking on her pink pearl. Her body jumps back, but Bryce pulls her back in towards him. Right in the middle of his face, as he continues to make love to her with his tongue. With all of her squirming and moaning, she yells out his name, just as she explodes right onto his tongue. Bryce sucks just about all of her creamy creations out of her, and then grabs her. Flipping her body over onto her stomach, pulling her ass up in the air. Her face down into the comforter blanket.

"You wanna feel daddy inside of you?"

Bryce speaks to her in her right ear. As he rubs the tip of himself up and down, inside of her soaking wet puddle from behind.

"Yes, baby, fuck me! I want every inch of you inside of me," she begged him.

Bryce fully inside of her, gripping a handful of curls and abusing her all in her middle, making it hurt just like she wanted it. They became wild animals – pulling, biting, and grabbing each other. Paris can no longer take it as Bryce continues to beat up her insides. She sinks her manicured nails into his back and his arms. She moans louder as she explodes, yelling out his name. "Aw Bryce!"

His teeth sink right into the back of her shoulder. Bryce finally reaches his goal, with a fist full of her curls, still in hand. Then they both fall weak, now into each other's arms.

Everything seems to be more than perfect, from someone on the outside looking into the new Frost family. That's who they were, and even though Bryce and Paris had just about everything in life, the foundation of their relationship was still a little shaky.

Which is what caused Paris's nerves to shift from side to side every now and then. She and Bryce would sometimes argue about marriage. He really wanted to be married to Paris. He was happy with her, and didn't desire to be with anyone else. Paris, on the other hand, was still battling with the past. Even though Bradley wasn't a great husband, the fact that she ran off with his brother made her wonder if they should even bother to get married.

However, that wasn't good enough for Bryce. Kalisha, who still lived in Austin, would often advise Paris to seek some type of counseling. Truth be told, Paris really hadn't healed from everything that she had taken in almost ten years ago. She would often try her best to block everything out of her mind, but it was just not possible. She really needed help. Especially with her being so distant with her first-born son.

"Baby, the kids are up now. I have to go into the office for a little while, and then go check on some things at the club," he whispered into her ear as she lay in bed, half-asleep and just as beautiful as ever. She opened her eyes and glimpsed him. She couldn't help but to smile, seeing how good he was looking.

"Will you be home for dinner? It's family night." She spoke softly, tugging at his left hand.

"I promise to make it home for family night," he grinned. "I love you, sweetheart." He kissed her on the lips one more time, and then walked out the door.

Easing her body out of bed, she headed to the shower, but her phone stops her from making her way into the bathroom. She started to ignore the phone call, but changed her mind when she saw Jermaine's name appear on her phone. Her best friend Kalisha's husband calling. Her eyebrow points straight up, wondering why he was calling her.

"Hey! What's up Jermaine?" Paris answered the phone, feeling somewhat confused.

"Hey Paris! Um I was wondering if you had talked to Kalisha anytime today or yesterday." He spoke with a worried tone.

Paris frowned with confusion, slipping on her robe, wondering what was going on. "I spoke with her a few days ago, when we were talking about getting together to take the kids to Disney World before school starts back. Is everything okay?"

"No, Paris. Everything is not okay. Kalisha is missing." His voice starts to tremble.

"What do you mean Kalisha is missing?" Paris tries not to yell, so the kids won't hear her and get scared.

Jermaine takes a deep breaths before he speaks again, trying his best not to break down. "She was supposed to pick up Corina from soccer practice," he said referring to their eight year old daughter. "Corina's coach called me saying that she had been sitting with her for about an hour, waiting on Kalisha to come, but she never showed up. So I left from my meeting at work and went and got Corina. We called Kalisha over and over, but her phone kept on going to voice-mail. Her truck was parked in the drive way, with the door wide open. After seeing that she was nowhere in the house, that's when I called the police. Now they're here, and they're treating me as if I have something to do with her disappearing. Paris you know that I love my wife, and I would never hurt her or bring any type of harm her way."

Jermaine can no longer hold it together; he breaks down on the phone. Paris tries her best to remain calm as tears start to streak down her face. She is in shock; her heart is sinking at the bottom of her stomach. Pacing back and forth, still trying to remain calm. Trying to search for words was causing her to break out into a sweat.

"Okay! Jermaine. Is there any sign of a struggle, or fight? Or have you and Kalisha been having any type of problems lately?"

His breaths heavy with tears, trying to collect his words, and thoughts. "I suspected that she could have been having an affair."

"What! Jermaine come on, why would you say something like that? Kalisha loves you and you know it. She wouldn't do anything like that. Besides if she did, she would have told me – I'm her best friend, and we tell each other everything." After Paris finished hissing at Jermaine, he was quiet for a couple of seconds, still taking deep breaths. "Hello, Jermaine are you there?"

"Yes, I'm still here. Now are you done yet?" His tone is now sharper than a knife.

"Yes! Speak your mind Jermaine," she replied

"Okay! Ms. Best friend. Well since the two of you share everything with each other, do you care to share with me about where she was at 2:00 am, coming in the house with her hair all over her damn head. Her make up smeared all over her face, with the smell of another man's fragrance. Did she tell you why there was a withdrawal of $5,000 from our savings account that she didn't care to inform me about. Me – her damn husband!" He yelled into the phone so loud, Corina started to cry.

"Daddy what's wrong? Why are these cops in our house? Where is mommy?" Eight year old Corina started to sob and cry, running into her daddy's arms.

"It's okay. Mommy will be home, honey." Jermaine takes Corina into his arms, holding her tight as he could.

Paris sat back down on the bed, trying to register the outburst that Jermaine had just delivered to her about her best friend. Now she was really at lost for words.

"Hello! Paris is you still there?" Jermaine spoke sarcastically.

"I'm still here," Paris slightly stuttered.

"Well do me a favor. When your best friend contacts you in any kind of way, please tell her to come home. I can live with the fact that she doesn't want to be married to me anymore, but I cannot live with the fact of her hurting my daughter."

At this point, Paris was becoming furious. She wanted to stick her hand through the phone and choke the life out of Jermaine.

"How dare you sit here and talk trash about my best friend – your wife at that – and you don't even know if she is dead or alive." She hissed. "You don't know what in the hell she is going through at this very moment Jermaine. It's like you don't even care!"

"Well, Paris I'm sorry that you feel that way. All I know is that lately my wife has been acting strange, coming home late, not wanting to be intimate with me, large amount of money missing out of our savings, and now all of sudden she is missing. Her car parked here, in our drive way. With her handbag sitting in the passenger seat, $300 cash with all her credit cards in her wallet, but her and the phone is gone. So! Like I said Paris! If you hear from her, or if you already know of her whereabouts. Please tell her to come back home, or at least call."

Just as Paris was about to say something, Jermaine hung up the phone, which really pissed her off. She started to call him back and cures him out, but she figured that wouldn't be a good idea. She was still trying to take into consideration that his wife was missing, and he really just wasn't himself. It was really not the time to be fighting with each other; this was the time for them to all come together. She scrolls through her phone to call Ms. Kathy. Kalisha's mother, but then she remembered was out of the country on a European Cruise. She called Bryce to inform him about the news that she just received, but no answer. Her mind was going 100 miles per an hour, with her pacing back and forth even more. Her concentration was broken by a knock at her bedroom door.

"Hey Mom, I'm back," B.J. said through the door. "Brielle and the twins want ice cream, I'm gonna get them a bowl of Cookies and Cream."

Paris tied her robe together, and ran to open the door as fast as she could, ready to start fussing. "No! You better not give them any ice – " She couldn't finish her sentence, though. She stopped in her tracks, as she flung the door open, seeing him standing there with his father's smile. She does her best to rush back into her room. Not able to look at him.

"Mom what's wrong?" B.J asked with his smile fading away.

"Nothing baby. I'm about to cook dinner, and I don't want the kids to spoil their appetite." She tries to hurry back in the room.

"Mom!"

"What is it, baby?"

"Why is it that every time you look at me, you act like you seen a ghost? You just act so weird every time I come around you." B.J looked straight into her eyes.

"B.J. I really need to go get into the shower. We can talk later." She hurried to shut the door, leaning her back against the wall. How much of this could she take? For years of her life, it's been one thing after another. She kept having visions of her ex-husband, and now her best friend was missing.

Tuesday August 11, 2015 1:15pm Austin, TX

Kalisha's nerves had been jumping up and down close to a week, ever since receiving an unwanted pop up visit from her past at the hospital where she worked as a Registered Nurse. She was falling apart, inside and out. Her body was only operating on two hours of sleep, with only meal supplement shakes in her system, due to lack out appetite. She wasn't able to function, let alone do her duties as a wife or a mother. The deep dark secret that she was carrying with her and that was about to make its way to the light was distracting her. She knew if her skeletons were to pop out of the closet, it would ruin her family. Her husband would definitely divorce her. She had held on to this secret for thirteen years, and it was beginning to unravel. Not even her mother, or her best friend knew about it. This past of hers has even showed up at her home, at her job, it has even showed up to a couple of Corina's soccer games. All she wanted was for this person to go away and never come back. However, she knew that wasn't going to happen.

"Hey Kalisha, you don't look so good. Are you okay?" asked Nurse Smith.

Kalisha closed her medical charts, turning to the kind old lady with sadness in her eyes. "I'm okay. I'm gonna go ahead and take off, so I can pick up Corina. I'll be back tomorrow morning," she said, walking off towards to nurse's station to grab her purse.

"Well, let me walk you to your car." Nurse Smith offered.

Kalisha was feeling somewhat annoyed, but was trying not to make it obvious, so she agreed to let Nurse Smith walk her outside.

"Kalisha. I don't mean to overstep my boundaries, but the other nurses and I are very worried about you. You really have not been yourself lately." Nurse Smith spoke with concern. Kalisha wasn't able to look her in the face without bursting into tears. She continued to shift her body from side to side. Then she managed to speak.

"Ms. Smith, I'm really dealing with some personal issues at the moment. I'm trying my best not to bring it inside of work, but I will be okay." Kalisha stated trying to fight back tears.

"My Dear, I'm sorry for everything that is going on, if you need to talk or anything, you know that I'm just a phone call away. I'm here if you need me, and I will be praying for you. Also, remember whatever troubles you are having. Just place it in God's hands, he will make a way. Call me if you need anything." Then she embraced her with a tight hug that caused Kalisha to let out a soft quiet cry.

"Are you going be okay to drive?"

Kalisha nodded and thanked her, walking through the hospital parking lot with her remote key in hand. Ready to unlock the door to her Black Infinity SUV. Soon as she arrives to her vehicle, there it was again. Her past stepping out of a parked all white 2008 Chevy Impala, parked right next to her. He stands about 6'2 with a milk chocolate complexion, and a nice shinny bald head. Sporting a pair of jeans, and a blue T- Shirt. He somewhat favored a black version of Mr. Clean.

"Well, well, well! Ms. Kalisha! I called you six times and you wouldn't answer your phone. See you done made me have to come back up to your job. You know that I'm really trying my best to be nice, but you on the other hand are not making that possible. Now come on, get in the car. Let's go back to the bank." He spoke with a friendly smile, but yet he was not a friendly person.

Kalisha froze up with her feet glued to the ground, a part of her wanted to scream so badly. Then she thought twice about it, when the man displayed the nine millimeter. In hand on his left side, to where only she could see it.

"Clint please go away, I have already given you five-thousand dollars," she began to cry. "The kind of money that you want, I don't have it."

"Look, Kalisha! You know where you can get the money from, so I suggest you make that phone call. Oh and by the way. Those tears don't faze me at all. You should have thought about that thirteen years ago, when your young stupid ass did what you did," he barked, trying his best not to get loud in the hospital parking lot.

"Why don't you just kill me, you rotten bastard!" She yelled so loud, a woman walking by with her baby shot her an ugly look. Then she crossed over to the other side of the parking lot.

"Okay Kalisha. You want to make a scene. Cool. I can meet up with your husband, at his office, and tell him all about his perfect little wife." He flashes a devilish smile.

Kalisha steps closer to him, and surprisingly reaching her hand all the way back to Mississippi, slaps the dog shit out of him. "Fuck you! Go to hell!" She stormed away from him, getting into her car. As he still stands there, wearing the same devilish smile on his face. Just as she starts to back up, with her SUV in reverse. Her heart drops when making eye contact, with the cinnamon color complexed little girl, with long brown jumbo curls. Sitting in the back seat. She couldn't help it; she had to roll her window down. Getting a full good look at her. Then she looks back at Clint, shaking her head in disbelief, shooting him a disgusting look.

"You are one twisted asshole!" She yelled out to him, from her car window.

"Yeah! Kalisha I may be a lot of things, but I'm nothing like the heartless bitch that you are. You just make sure you contact me when you get my money." He gave her an evil look.

He put on a pair of black shades and walks over to his car, jumps in and speeds off. Kalisha's heartbeat speeds up so fast, she thought that her heart was going to jump right out of her chest. She was a nervous wreck and didn't know what to do with herself. This guy had her so messed up in the head; she had even considered taking a bottle of Secobarbital from the medication room, so she could end her own life. She felt trapped and was not able to take it any longer, regret and guilt was eating her alive. If she was able to turn back the hands on the clock, and do things different. Then that's exactly what she would do. However that was just not possible at all.

Driving up the access road of Mopac and Parmer, after speeding out of the hospital parking lot. Kalisha's phone starts to vibrate in the pocket of her baby blue scrub nurse uniform. She starts to shake when she see that it is Clint calling.

"WHAT THE HELL DO YOU WANT?" She screams into the phone.

"You passed up the bank bitch, now turn back around. I'm right behind you." He spoke so harsh and cold into the phone.

Kalisha wanted to piss on herself when she saw Clint following behind her, in her rear view mirror. She knew that it was about to be that time for her to pick up Corina from soccer practice, and she did not have time to play speed chase with Clint. She approaches a red light, with Clint still on her tail. Her palms start to sweat, and so does her forehead. When noticing there were no other cars coming from the next enter section over, who had the green light. Kalisha carefully sped her way through the red light, making the first right turn, and then cutting through one of the subdivisions. She turned onto a street where she spotted a library, and decided to pull in immediately. Parking in between a white minivan, and a black ford expedition. She felt somewhat safe at the moment. Due to the fact that Clint could not take the chance on getting pulled over, with a gun on him, and a child in the car. Grabbing for her phone to call her husband Jermaine, to tell him to pick up Corina from soccer practice, because she was running late. Just as she clicked on his name, her phone powers off. Due to her dead battery. She starts to loose herself. Screaming at the top of her lungs, kicking, and beating the steering wheel with her fist. As tears pour out nonstop.

"OH GOD JUST TAKE ME NOW!" she cried out so loud, covering up her eyes.

As bad as her heart was hurting, and her mind was so screwed up. She had to calm herself down, and do some quick thinking for a plan. After thirty minutes passed by, Kalisha made her way to her home. Planning to pack up some clothes for her and her family so they could leave out of Austin. She planned on confessing everything to Jermaine, regardless if he decided to leave her or not. There was no way she could continue to go on in life this way, especially holding the secret that could tear her marriage apart.

Finally making her way to the house. Just as Kalisha placed both feet onto the ground, as she stepped out of her SUV. A tight painful grip was formed around her wrist, with a metal object pointed into the right side of her waist. It didn't take her long to figure out that it was Clint pushing his nine miller meter into her waist.

"Don't even think about it, BITCH. If you scream I will blow a fucking hole in your waist. Now come on. Let's go get in the car, and don't make a scene in front of my baby girl. Or I'm gonna put your triflin ass in the trunk, and I know you don't want that because we have a long ride ahead of us." He spoke through his clenched teeth.

"Clint where are you taking me?" She started to cry.

"We are going for a long drive, now sit down, and buckle the hell up!" He threw Kalisha down into the passenger seat, placed her seat belt on. Then he pulled out a set of shackled handcuffs. Cuffing her hands and ankles together as if she was a prisoner.

"I hope you didn't drink a lot of water today, because I'm not stopping for no bathroom breaks." He slammed the door, and then got into the driver seat.

"Daddy, where are we going? Who is this lady?" The frightened little girl in the backseat asked in a whimpering voice.

Clint puts on his seat belt and turns back to look at the little girl in the backseat. "Sit back sweetheart. We are going to a little family reunion."

Chapter Thirteen

Bryce sat back in his Italian leather chair as his eyes scanned through the well put together office. Thanks to his assistant, April Kendall. He was blessed to be where he was at in life, and he knew it —even though he and Paris' relationship didn't come from the best foundation. As Bryce continued to write his brother and put money on his books, he never mentioned to Bradley at all about being a father, but he still sent pictures to him of B.J and Brielle. He made sure to just send pictures of those two only – leaving out Paris and the twins.

Another thing that would always put Bryce in deep thought is that he really wanted to be legally married to Paris. Although they both carried the last name Frost, because Paris kept her last name after she divorced Bradley, that was not good enough for Bryce. Every time he would bring up the subject about them getting married, Paris would disregard it, along with his feelings. Or she would say there was no reason for them to fix something that wasn't broken. He truly loved Paris, and wanted to be with only her.

Bryce snaps out of his deep thoughts, when April knocks at the door. She stands about 5'7 with a slender frame, big chocolate brown eyes, creamy vanilla skin, a pixie haircut, and a set of full pouty lips. She carried a Swedish accent, but you were still able to understand her while carrying on a conversation with her. April's mother, Kimberly, moved to New York City from Sweden, and hooked up with a pimp by the name of Raymond Kendall. Everyone called him R.K.

He spotted Kimberly coming out of a Harlem bookstore one day; he knew right off the back that she was from out of town. Not too many white people shopped in that area, especially back in the 70's. When R.K approached Kimberly, the minute she spoke back to him, he immediately knew right off the rip that she was from another country. Judging from her Swedish accent. He was so amazed by her long straight blond hair, and ocean blue eyes. Not because he was attracted to her, it was because he knew that she would make him a lot of money. If he was able to sweet talk her into working for him as one of his girls, that's exactly what he did, and he succeeded. She became his number one money maker; she was bringing him in a surplus of cash, every night before midnight had arrived. Everything was going so sweet, until Kimberley informed R.K that she was pregnant. He instantly flew off the handle, yelling at her about not using protection with her tricks. Then she had to shut him up with the quickness, when letting him know that she never slept with none of her tricks. Her head game was so good; her tricks would pay her as if she spent the whole night with them. One night R.K got a little curious about the piece of white chocolate that he had on his team, as the Jack Daniels flowed through his system. That was the night he broke one of the most important rules of the Pimp Game. Sleeping with one of his working girl, and especially without protection. After April was born, Kimberly packed up and moved to Houston, TX. She wanted to start over and give April a better life. April was a damn good worker. She had

Bryce's back to the fullest, but it was one problem that somewhat hindered their work relationship. Paris could not stand the ground that April walked on, and she hated that Bryce worked side by side with her on a daily basis. She handled a lot of business for Bryce when it came to his real estate company, and the night club he opened called Classics. So they had to be around each other all the time, and it made Paris sick to her stomach. For some reason she felt that April wanted Bryce.

"Hey April! Come on in, how is everything going?" Bryce greeting her with a friendly welcome.

"Hello Bryce! I complete all of the paperwork for the staff at the club, and a lady name Jennifer Moss called about the property over by the Hobby Airport," she stated as she places some documents on his desk.

"Thank you. Did you get a chance to do any interviews for the security positions over at the club?" He asked as he stapled some paperwork together.

"Yes I did two interviews. The first guy I'm not really sure about. The second guy, I feel like he is more qualified for the position. I'm meeting with him again for a second interview on Thursday."

Bryce nodded his head yes, letting her know that he was satisfied with her response. Just as he was about to hand April a list of things to complete, the front office door flings open. April immediately stands to her feet, when noticing Paris walking in at full speed. The look on April's face let Bryce know that she was about to haul ass, but it was too late to run. Paris had already stormed in with a nasty attitude, before April could even get out of the door.

Brushing right past her, wearing a mad as hell look on her face.

"Hello Paris. How are you doing?" April nervously stuttered with her Swedish Accent, looking like a frighten little girl.

Paris rolled her eyes at April, without speaking to her, walking into Bryce's direction behind his desk. April immediately grabbed her paperwork and notes, practically running out of the office. Soon as the door closed, Bryce turned to Paris. Ready to address her rude behavior. However, he wasn't able to, because Paris wasted no time at all going in on him.

"I tried to call you and you didn't answer your phone, every time her ass is around you never pick up." Paris barked at him.

"Look Paris this is not the time or the place. Don't do this hear at my place of business. What is going on?" Bryce trying his best to keep calm.

"Jermaine called me saying that Kalisha is missing. She didn't pick up Corina from soccer practice, and her car was parked in the driveway with the driver door wide open." She stated as she took deep breaths.

Bryce can't believe his ears; he jumps up out of his chair, just as confused as Paris is.

"What do you mean she is missing? When was the last time he talked to her?"

Paris eyes starts to water up with tears. She can no longer speak; all she could do was cry. Hoping and praying that her best friend was alive and okay. She continued to replay her and Jermaine's conversation over and over in her head. Some of the stuff that he was saying did not make any sense, but most of all it just didn't sound like Kalisha. She continued to pray to God that her friend was not harmed in any kind of way.

"Okay! Baby first let's pray that she is okay. We probably should make our way to Austin, so we can be there for Jermaine during all of this. I'm pretty sure he is going crazy not knowing where his wife is at." Bryce speaks to Paris as he holds her in his arms, trying to calm her down.

"Bryce I just don't understand. How is it that Kalisha is all of sudden missing? But yet her purse was left sitting in the car with money, and credit cards in it. Something is definitely wrong with this picture. Then Jermaine was saying how he believed that she was having an affair." Paris explains as she sniffles.

Wrinkles of a frown appeared on Bryce's forehead, along with a blank stare. None of it was making any type of sense to him at all.

"Um Baby. Why don't we call your dad and ask him to stay over with the kids. So we can drive up to Austin, Jermaine really needs us there." Bryce suggested.

Right when Paris got ready to reply, there was a knock at the door. Once Bryce spoke the words come in; here comes April walking in. With the same scared look on her face, from when Paris had arrived. She really tried her best to keep her distance from Paris whenever she was around, but she had to interrupt for a very important phone call that she wasn't able to take a message.

"Excuse me Bryce. I'm sorry to disturb you guys, but you have a very important phone call."

April spoke. Handing Bryce the cordless phone, and trying to hurry up and get out Paris's sight.

Awkwardness filled the room instantly. Bryce already knew who was on the phone, when April walked in with it. Whenever that cordless phone would ring, he knew it could only be two people to call that phone. Due to the fact he had the extra line installed, for only two particular callers. His mother Gloria Frost and his brother Bradley Frost. Calling from prison. The reason he had the extra lined installed at the real estate office, was so he wouldn't have to talk to them in front of Paris. He knew how she felt about them both, so he did the best he could to keep the distance between them. Then to he didn't want to take the chance of his mom and brother finding out about him and Paris's relationship.

"Hello Mom! How are you doing? Bryce spoke into the phone, trying his best to hurry up and walk out of the office. So Paris didn't have to be around while he carried on the conversation with his mother. Not only just his mother. Yet the woman who was responsible for Paris's mother's death. Paris immediately snatched her purse from Bryce's desk and headed for the door to storm out. Until Bryce blocked her from walking out, still trying to maintain the phone call with his mother.

"Let me go Bryce! I'm not going to sit here and listen to you talk to the monster who had my mother killed." She hissed at him, she was trying to say it loud enough on purpose so Gloria could hear her. Bryce made sure he pressed the mute button on the cordless phone, so she wouldn't hear anything Paris was saying.

"Look Baby please calm down, just let me see if she needs anything. This is why I have her and Bradley to call the office phone instead of my own personal phone, because I know how you feel about the two of them. Sweetie you have got to understand, she is still my mother and she is in prison. I'm the only one who is around to look out for her." Bryce pleaded with Paris, with tears welling up in his eyes.

Paris stopped with her tantrum for a couple of seconds, and then backed away from Bryce. Anger appeared on her face, as her nostrils started to flare up.

"Now you listen to me. I don't have to understand shit when it comes to that bitch, or that treacherous ass brother of yours. Your mother and brother made my life a living hell, and to tell you the truth I don't even know why they are still on this earth breathing. They are only just taking up space."

Bryce was really thrown off by Paris's last statement, standing there speechless. Even though he understood why she hated his mother so much, but he had never known for Paris to wish death on anybody.

"Paris. Go to the house and pack up, so we can drive out to Austin. Jermaine really needs us there." He spoke calmly as he could.

"No! What I'm going to do is go over to my father's house, and talk to him about what's going on. If you are not ready to roll out in a couple of hours, then I will be going to Austin without you" Then she stormed out of Bryce's office slamming the door.

Bryce could not believe how cold she spoke to him. He had never seen her this way; this was a totally different Paris that he was looking at. Although he did understand where she was coming from, when it came to his mother Gloria. What his mother did wasn't his fault, and yes she was the one who had Paris's mother killed. However at the end of the day, it was still his duty to look after his mother, while she was serving her time in prison. The only thing he wanted was to keep the peace, and be there for the two women that he loved and cared about. So that was one of the reasons for him getting the second phone line installed at the office, and the other reason was so there would be no type of indication that Bryce and Paris were together. It was to remain on the hush from Gloria and Bradley that Bryce was even a father period.

After Paris left out of the office he continued on with the phone call from his mother.

"Hey Mom! How are you doing?"

"I'm holding up baby, just been keeping God close. You know I would like to get a visit from you, I understand that you are a very busy man. However it would be nice to see you." She spoke so soft and tenderly.

"Yeah Mom. I do plan on making my way there as soon as possible. Just got a lot going on."

"Okay Son. Whenever you get time, I would love to see you. Now they are about to do count, I have to go. I love you."

"I love you mom."

Bryce pressed the end button on the cordless phone, trying to hold back tears. It really broke his heart that his mother was in prison, although he knew why she was in there. He still never wanted her to be locked up; he of all people knew how that was. After over nine years he still hadn't went to see his mother, the only time Gloria got to see the visiting room was when she was cleaning it up after, after visitation hours were over. Bryce made a mental note to himself to stop by the nearest place that had Money Gram service, so he could send off the monthly $400 through J-Pay for Gloria and Bradley. Just as he was shutting down his computer, April knocked at the door poking her head in.

"Bryce I really need to talk to you." She stated straight forward, with a stern look on her face.

"Yes April. What's up?" Bryce replied gathering up his belongings.

"Okay this thing with your wife needs to stop. She is very rude and disrespectful to me, and I don't know why she doesn't like me. I have done nothing but be kind to her, and yet she treats me like some step child." April spoke in her frustrated accent.

Bryce turned his head with a smile on his face, trying his best not to laugh. He didn't turn fast enough, because April caught it and got upset. Playfully throwing a paper clip at him.

"Stop it Bryce! Not Funny!" She pouted stomping her foot down.

She thought that Bryce was laughing at her accent, because he laughed every time she got upset. This time he wasn't laughing at her. He was smiling because it sounded good him, to hear someone address Paris as his wife. April doesn't know the history with Bryce and Paris, she just assumed like everyone else that she was his wife, and all four kids belonged to both of them.

"Okay April. I'm sorry. I will talk to her, but right now we have to make our way to Austin. Something is going on with a close friend of ours, and I just know that this I-10 traffic is not going to be nothing nice. When all of this is over, I will definitely talk to Paris. You're right; she should not be treating you this way. You have done nothing wrong to her. You are a great assistant and I don't wanna lose you." He spoke with compassion.

Making his way to the door, so he could get going. The cordless phone rings again. He started to ignore it, and just let it ring, but then decided not to.

"Hello?"

"You have a collect call from TDC Inmate Bradley Frost. Press #1 to accept this call. Press #2 to decline this call." The recorded operator spoke on the other end.

"Hey Bradley! How are you doing bro?" Bryce spoke rolling his eyes.

"I don't know little bro. You tell me, haven't heard from you in a while." Bradley replied back in a sarcastically manner.

"Well I know you get the $400 a month that I send to you. So don't act as if I just disappeared off the face of the earth. Which is way more than what you have ever done for me?"

"Well, look man. Is there any way you can get in touch with Paris? I really want to see my kids. You used to send me pictures of them all the time, but then you stopped. Not sure why, but hey. It is what it is."

"I will see what I can do, but right now I'm in the middle of something. I will try my best to contact Paris. At the end of the day she has the say so, and I'm not trying to step on anybody's toes. You feel me, bro?"

"Yeah man whatever. Just do that for me if you can, please? Whenever you talk to mom again tell her that I love her." Then Bradley hung up. After all this time of him been locked up, he was still an arrogant ungrateful bastard.

Bryce reached into the bottom drawer of his desk, pulled out a bottle of Scotch, and a shot glass that he purchased from the Brazil Gift Shop. During one of him and Paris's vacation trips. After gulping down two shots, he was ready to be on his way. He really needed it after receiving the horrible news about Kalisha, and he knew Paris was gonna be raising some type of hell. Sometimes he felt like he couldn't win for loosing. Here it was he wanted to legally be married to Paris. The woman that he loved so much, but the history with their family was standing in the way. Not that Bryce was bothered by it at all; he was remaining quiet about everything because that's what Paris wanted. Other than that he could really careless. Even if Paris did agree to go ahead and marry Bryce, before she was able to do so. The first thing she needed to do was seek professional help. She may not have notice it, but her attitude and mood swings were all over the place. Not to mention the disconnection with her son B.J. It was really sad that she could not look at her son for too long, or be around him in the same room for too long. Her emotions would get the best of her, and she was never able to handle it.

Bryce thought back to three months prior, on Mother's Day. Paris kicked, tossed and turned the whole night, and early that morning. As if she was having a horrible dream, it was like the devil had gotten a hold of her. Bryce rolled over to wake her up, wiping her forehead with a wash cloth. Her lavender gown was drenched with her sweat, her eyes blood shot red. Once he woke her up, she drifted off back to sleep in his arms. Bryce was up within a couple of hours after that. He made his way to the kitchen, to prepare a nice Mother's Day breakfast for Paris. Bryce instructed B.J to serve the breakfast to his mother in bed, while he, Brielle, and the twins set up her gifts on the dining room table. After B.J set the plate of Pancakes, Turkey Sausage, and Eggs on the night stand next to the bed. He bends down to place a soft kiss on his mother's cheek. The minute his lips touched her cheek, Paris jumped up out of nowhere. Screaming and crying at the top of her lungs.

She almost hit poor B.J in the face, but he was able to jump back fast enough. Even when he was trying to calm her down and reassure her that she was okay, and that it was just him – her son. He took her in his arms, and she still continued to cry her eyes out. Once Bryce entered into the room, B.J left out. In fact he stayed in his room the whole day, not wanting to come out. Even after Paris calmed down, and begged him to come out of his room. He still wouldn't budge. B.J actually felt like he did something wrong, and he felt like he ruined Mother's Day. From then on Bryce and Kalisha had talked to Paris about seeking professional help, especially if it was affecting her and her son's relationship. At the end of the day, it was up to Paris to get help if she really wanted to. No one could make her do it.

Chapter Fourteen

Paris walked into her the office of her place of business
– Frost Group Home Service – that she started up a few
years back. After Nursing School she decided to go into
business for herself, instead of working at a hospital or a
doctor's office. However she really didn't have to work, she
was still sitting on a nice amount of money she had left
over. Not to mention she also invested in property that was
bringing her a nice amount in every month. That wasn't
even included what Bryce was making. She was financially
set, with or without Bryce. She answered some emails,
completed some paperwork. Then walked into the other
office of her Assistant Brittney. Brittney stands about 5'2,
very petite, with short natural curly hair. With a sweet and
sensitive personality. With an assistant like Brittney, Paris
barley had to lift a finger to do anything. She had and kept
everything on point for Paris and her group home business.

"Hello Paris, how are you doing today?" Brittney spoke
in a soft tender voice.

"Hey Brittney! I'm okay. Look I have to go to Austin for
a family emergency, so I will be out for the rest of this
week. Are you going to be okay to hold everything down?"
Paris stated as she leaned up against the open office door.

"Sure, Paris. Is there anything else you need for me to
do?" Brittney asked standing up.

"No. That's about it, and Joyce will be the nurse on call
for this week."

"Okay Paris. I hope and pray that everything is okay in Austin." Brittney said as she pushed her glasses up to her face.

"Thank you Brittney."

Paris collected a few more items from her office, and then left out of the building to head home. Pulling into the driveway, she noticed her sister London's Baby Blue Audi parked in the driveway. She was so happy that her sister came over right away, when she called to inform her about Kalisha being missing. He father Jamaican George had just sent a text message saying that he was on his way. Soon as Paris stepped foot into the house, London ran up to her in tears to embrace her. Even though it was Kalisha and Paris who were best friends, London still loved Kalisha just like she was her own sister.

"You still haven't heard from her?" London asked, crying up a storm.

"No. I haven't honey. Her phone keeps going to voice mail. Where are the kids?" Paris asked her sister, trying her best not to cry.

"Oh the twins and Brielle are out in the backyard playing with Pebbles, and B.J is in his room." London replied, wiping her tears away.

Paris knocked on B.J door, but he wouldn't answer. So she tried to open it by turning the knob, but it was locked.

"B.J! Open the door I need to talk to you!" She spoke loud into the crack of the door.

"Oh! Now you wanna talk to me. Just go away, you have your three other kids to talk to." He yelled out to her.

"Bradley Frost Jr. If you don't open up this door, I'm gonna kick it down!" She screamed so loud, London came running to see what was going on.

B.J swung the door open, now standing face to face with his mother. Looking her dead in the eye. She tries to turn away, but he grabs her. Holding her tight.

"B.J let go of me!" She yells, trying to break away from his tight grip. Paris must have forgotten that she did not have a typical wimpy thirteen year old kid. B.J was very tall and active for his age. He was even hitting the weights each time after playing basketball at the gym. So Paris calmly spoke to him again.

"B.J let me go. I'm not asking you, I am telling you." Paris turns her head not making eye contact.

"Mom all I want you to see is that I am not him. I know why you can't look at me, or why you can't stand to be in the same room with me for too long. Mamas please love me like you love Brielle and the twins. Don't run away when I walk into the same room as you. Mama I am not him! I may look like him but I am not him. Mama I love you." B.J tears up so bad, but he never loosens his grip on his mother.

Paris still gripped into B.J's arms; she tries her best not to look at him. She closes her eyes as tight as she can, still trying to break away from him. She opens her eye with tears rolling out to see London and Bryce standing there with sadness in their eyes.

"Dammit Bryce will you get him off of me, the two of you just gonna stand there like dumb asses and let him grab me. Get him off of me now!!!!" Paris screams out so loud, crying like a child throwing a tantrum. London walks over to try and grab B.J, but Bryce gently grabs London's hand stopping her.

"No London. I'm sorry sweetie, but she needs to hear him out. You don't know how things are between them day to day. He is not going to hurt her." Bryce spoke calmly to her.

London backed off, and continued to watch her nephew and sister, with their hurtful cries. She couldn't take it anymore, she ran off into the living room crying her eyes out.

Bryce walked over to B.J and Paris.

"Paris. Baby you have got to hear him out, B.J is crying out for your love. He needs his mother, he is not his father. Hold him; tell him how much you love him."

She continues to cry, with her eyes closed tight. After a couple of seconds she finally opens them, crying even more when she looks directly into B.J's eyes. He loosen his grip, she grabs him into her arms, holding him. Crying nonstop.

"See Mama! I told you I'm not him, I'm your son, and I, love you." B.J and Paris wrapped into each other's arms. As they stand there holding each other the knock at the door interrupts them.

"B.J Honey I'm so sorry. Please forgive me baby" Paris said to B.J. Looking into his eyes. London yelled out to Bryce from the door.

"Bryce! April your assistant is here."

Paris immediately whips her head around, and fallow Bryce to the door. She completely forgot that she and her son just shared an emotional breakdown, but oh no she wasn't having it. She wanted to know why in the hell was

April knocking at their door, and she better had a damn good reason.

"Hey April! What's going on?" Bryce asked walking to the door, where April was standing.

"Bryce I tried to call you, but you didn't answer. I'm sorry to show up at your home like this, but it's very important." April spoke nervously.

Paris stares at her with an evil look, wanting to punch her in the face.

"Don't you know that we are in the middle of a family crisis? What is it that is so important to where you had to bring your raggedy ass to our home?" Paris screaming and walking up on April at the same time.

"Paris calm down, what are you doing?" London ran over to Paris, trying to take her by the arm.

"No! London let me go! This stank bitch has no idea that I can see right through her, and that fake ass accent of hers. She is after my husband, and I'm about to beat the dog shit out of her, for her showing up to my doorstep." Paris runs up to April, charging at her with her right fist. She doesn't succeed because Bryce bear hugs her into a corner.

"Paris stops it right now! I told you that I don't want nobody else but you! Just stop it!" Bryce yelled into her face, somewhat calming her down. "So I'm your husband now? Huh?"

April hesitantly walks into to Bryce's direction, with a worried look on her face.

"Bryce, the warden from the prison called. Your mother was rushed to the hospital, she had a stroke."

Bryce loosens his grip on Paris, turning his attention to April. With sadness in his eyes, he is lost for words. His heart making its way to pop right out of his chest. Regardless of what his mother did, he stilled loved her. Paris pushes Bryce out of the way, walking right over to April. Giving her a good full force push with both hands, causing April to fly across the room, falling onto the floor.

"You brought your ass all the way over here to my house, to deliver some news about his mama. Now that shit could have waited, we got bigger issues over here. Get your ass out of my house." Paris made an attempt to kick April while she was lying on the floor. Out of nowhere London comes running up to Paris, screaming and cursing at her.

"Paris what the fuck is wrong with you! You really need to get some damn help, something is seriously wrong with you." London screamed helping April up off the floor. Paris gives her sister a confused look, she didn't understand why London was defending April, and she didn't even know her. Most of all, why was she going against her own sister.

April gets up, dusting off her Pink KLS skirt, with a slight grin on her face. Walking over to Paris with her hand on her hip.

"It's seemed to me that your sister has not had the conversation with you yet, and I really wish she would. I am sick and tired of you disrespecting me; I have not done anything but be nice to you. For the record Paris Frost, I don't want Bryce. I don't like DEEK!" April yelled in her strong accent, causing Paris to give her a wired look frowning at her.

"You don't like what?" Paris yelled.

April repeated herself in more of a yelling tone, sounding clearer.

"I SAID THAT I DON'T LIKE DICK!"

London immediately walks over standing by April's side.

"Look Paris. When we had lunch today, I was trying my best to tell you this, but it was hard for me. I mean I had a hard time accepting myself, but just to let you know. She doesn't want Bryce, April is my girlfriend, and yes I am gay. I was the one who introduced her to Bryce, when he started up both of his businesses. That's how she got the job to be his assistant. So when I would hear you go on and on about this girl name April, who was after Bryce. I came close to telling you, but I would always chicken out." London steps closer to April, holding her by the waist.

Paris stands there with her holding her chest, with her mouth so wide open. She can't believe her ears or eyes. Looking over at Bryce noticing that he was in his own little sad world, sitting down on the love seat. Trying to collect his thoughts, with his head buried into both of his hands. She turns back to look at London and April, them still standing in front of her hugging each other. B.J appears by his mother's side, taking her by the hand.

"Mom are you okay?" He asked with concern.

Paris shakes her head, in shock not knowing what to say. Just as she turns to walk away. Her phone rings. She is somewhat relieved when she see Kalisha's name pop up on her phone.

"Oh My God! Kalisha Honey are you okay?" Paris screams into the phone, as Bryce and London run over to her. There is no respond on the other end.

"Hello! Kalisha Sweetie Talk To Me! Hello!"

The phone goes dead, reading lost call. Paris dials her number back, but all she gets is Kalisha's voice mail. She continues to call back over and over. Out of fear and frustration, she breaks down to the floor, screaming and crying. Still trying to call Kalisha back, and the calls still going straight to voice mail. London sits next to her on the floor, taking her sister into her arms.

"Why does this keep happening to me? The people in my life that I love so much, keeps getting taken away from me!" She screams out, with tears.

The twins Braylon and Brianna, Brielle come running in from the backyard, when hearing their mother's cries.

"Mommy what's wrong? Why are you crying?" They both asked sounding like they were about to start crying themselves.

"Mommy just need to get some rest, she is not feeling good."

Bryce said as he took both twins over to B.J, pulling April to the side.

"April could you please do me a favor? Take the kids with you for a little while; this is all too much for them to see." Bryce pulled out two hundred dollars handing it to her. He knew that it wasn't in April's job description to watch over his kids, and especially at the last minute.

"Bryce, just let the kids stay over at my place for the night. It really looks like you and Paris have a lot going on, and you guys really need time together. By the way I don't want your money, London's family is my family." She smiled at him, walking away to the kids' room to pack them an overnight bag.

Bryce heart instantly started to melt; he didn't know what he would do without April. After the kids went into the living room, giving their mother and Auntie London good bye kisses. Paris stood to her feet with tears in her eyes, as she apologized to April, and then thanked her for taking the kids. Bryce went into his study, so he could make some phone calls about what was going on with his mother. He prayed to himself that she was going to be fine. Paris turns to London sitting by her side on the couch, still not knowing what to say. London got ready to speak, but Paris's musical ring tone intervened. She noticed Jermaine's name popping up on the phone.

"Hey Jermaine! Has she tried to call you?" Paris asked so desperately.

"No the hell she didn't call. But know this; your so called best friend has a secret that I'm pretty sure you would like to hear. I broke into Kalisha's private safe that I didn't know anything about, that's hidden in her garden house. I have some disturbing information about your friend. Would you care to hear?"

Paris was now pissed.

"You know what Jermaine, fuck you! My friend is missing and you don't even care, I'm starting to feeling like you had something to do with her disappearing!" Paris yelled into the phone, and then she hung up.

"What the hell was that all about?" London asked.

"Girl, Jermaine is really tripping, he is acting like he don't even care that Kalisha is missing. I don't think it's a good idea for us to go to Austin, he is really acting crazy." Paris said as she flopped back down on the couch next to London.

Wednesday August 12, 2015 7:45am Houston, TX Gulf Inn Hotel

It was a very long and fearful night for Kalisha. She had been living a horrible nightmare, and she wanted someone to pinch her, so she could wake up. However, it was a horrible reality for her. At this point she just wanted to die, she just wished that this Clint character from her past would kill her and get it over with. There was no way in hell he was going to make it that easy for her. She had the longest five hour drive to Houston. Shackled down in the car with Clint, and this preteen girl.

Clint pulled into the parking lot of the hotel in Houston, TX around 6:15pm the day before. He checked into two different hotel rooms, one for his daughter, and the other one for him and Kalisha with a double bed. After Clint checked in at the front desk, he made his way back to the car. With Kalisha stilled cuffed and shackled, and his daughter in the back seat. He instructed his daughter to go to her hotel room, and dragged Kalisha to their room. He ordered a pizza and let Kalisha feed herself, while stilled handcuffed at the small table in the room. He continued to ask her over why did she make him do this, and why did she ignore him when he asks her for help. Her only reply to his questions was: Just Kill Me. When Clint grew tired of it, he just chained her to the bed, and then he got into the other bed, and went to sleep. So he could proceed with his mission.

The next morning at 7:45am, Kalisha felt a painful slap on the right side of her face, with Clint standing over her. "Rise and shine, bitch!" he barked at her.

Kalisha let out a silent cry, really the girl was all cried out. She had been crying from Austin to Houston, and then cried all night. Clint took her phone, and powered it on with his charger plugged into the wall.

"Now you listen here, you fucking whore. I want you to get the address and log it into the navigation system. We are all the way here in Houston, so I strongly advise you to do as I say. Or I will not hesitate to beat the living shit out of you. So here log it in." Clint spoke so cold and heartless.

Kalisha did as she was told. Then he snatched the phone from her, sitting it on the table to charge. He looked at her with disgust, and hate. Kalisha sits on the side of the bed still shackled down, in her scrub uniform. She desperately needed a bath, and her hair was all over the place. Clint turned the television on, with the News Station talking about the weather. Kalisha limps to the bathroom still handcuffed. After she comes back out, sitting on the bed. Clint out of nowhere jumps up, shouting at the top of his lungs, "Ain't this bout a bitch?"

Kalisha jumps and falls off the bed, struggling to get back up. She is in complete shock, when she looks up to see her picture on the News for being missing. Her driver's license picture was displayed across the television. She could not take her eyes off the T.V. Clint walks grab the remote, to cut off the T.V.

"Well, looks like you're a celebrity now. They got your picture all over the news in different places. Looks like we are not leaving out of here until tonight when it's dark. So you can lie back down, and make yourself comfortable." Clint spoke sarcastically.

"Clint, I feel sick." Kalisha spoke while holding her stomach. He turns to her with a grin on his face.

"Yeah! I bet. You might be hungry, maybe you should walk down the street to Burger King. Since you like to have everything your way." He burst into a devilish laugh.

Kalisha lay down to cry more tears, she knew this was going to be a long day and a long night for her. She was having all different types of regret, from her past. Never in a million years would she have thought that it would catch back up to her this way. She prayed for God to just come and take her now, she no longer wanted to live. Turning her head to the right, she notice that Clint was dosing off with the nine millimeter lying next to his side. As she ease up from the bed, stilled cuffed and all. Snatches the gun, placing it into her mouth, pulling the trigger. However all she gets is clicking noise from the gun. Clint jumps out of bed, giving her a good slap to the face, snatching the gun from her.

"So you really don't want to face your problems, or your past. You rather take your own life. You selfish bitch! You not even thinking about your daughter at home in Austin." Clint yelled into her face.

He takes the gun, grabs the clip from his bag, and then loads it up. "Now it's really loaded and if you try anything else. I will bust a cap in your fucking leg." He pressed the gun into her knee.

Chapter Fifteen

Bryce walked into the bedroom, sitting on the side that Paris was on. Watching her sleep. He loved her so much; he could not imagine his life without her. That's why he was sitting waiting for her to wake up, so they could talk. She was sleeping so good, due to the fact the night before was crazy. So she had every right to be tired. She rolled over to feel for Bryce's side of the bed, noticing that he wasn't there. As she sat up, she smiled when seeing him sitting there. Watching her as he was looking good in his yellow Ralph Lauren Polo Shirt, and Ralph Lauren Jeans.

"Good morning sleeping beauty." He spoke with a smile.

Paris crawled over to him, with a big smile. Hugging him from his side. She loved waking up to him every morning; it was no doubt that she loved Bryce.

"Are you hungry?" He asked, kissing her on the forehead.

"A little. When is April bringing the kids back?"

"Oh the twins where having such a ball, April decided to take them to Kemah Board Walk. So is it okay if she brings them back tomorrow?"

"Yeah I guess." She replied, stepping out of bed.

Bryce and Paris sat down at the table, ready to dig in their French toast, Eggs, and Turkey Bacon. Paris sipped her freshly squeezed orange juice, grabbing the remote to turn on the kitchen flat screen that was hanging above the table. Bryce cleared his throat.

"Paris. Honey I'm kind of glad that we have this time alone, we really need to talk."

"About what?" She replied, flipping through the channels.

"Paris I love you so much, and I want things to be right between us, and our family that we have. I know that we both carry the last name Frost, but baby I want to be married to you. I do understand the situation with you and my brother, but hell we been living together as a family for damn near ten years now. So why not be married, eventually my brother will find out about us. You know that he is not going to be in prison forever, and he is gonna want to see B.J and Brielle. All I'm saying is that I don't want us to be in the dark anymore. Please let's make this right Paris."

She sits in silent for a couple of minute, taking in everything Bryce just poured out to her. She loved him also, but before Paris did anything, she really needed to get professional help.

"Bryce I'm stilled messed up about a lot of things that has happened, I don't want to marry you and then you will be ready to divorce me a year or two later. Just because I'm so screwed up. I love you so much, I can't imagine life without you baby." she replied.

"Baby we can fix it. I actually called this lady name Angela Jackson. She is a family therapist, and I hear that she is great at what she do. Whatever needs to be fixed, I'm willing to go through it with you. I'm by your side all the way, when you hurt, I hurt. We can do this together for the both of us and our family."

Paris shakes her head agreeing.

"Okay sweetie. I'm willing to get the help." She slightly smiled.

"I love you Paris."

"I love you, too, Bryce." She blew him a kiss, and then turned her attention to the T.V.

"Oh shit! Baby, look! Kalisha's picture is on the news!" She screamed, pointing up at the flat screen.

They both pushed their plates to the side, and remained focused on the news. A tear fell from Paris's right eye, she thought about calling Jermaine back, but then decided not to. When thinking about how she cursed him out the night before. Although she was somewhat curious about what he had to tell her, when he mentioned that Kalisha had a secret. Most of all she was just worried if her best friend was okay.

"Baby let's just give it to God, she has got to be okay." Bryce walked over to her, holding her in his arms, as she cried.

The doorbell ringed, Bryce jogged over to answer it.

"Hey London! What's going on, sis?" He greeted London with a hug, as she walked in the door.

"What's up, bro!" she smiled.

"Is my sister okay? Is she mad at you for not telling her about me and April?"

"Yeah she good... she's in the kitchen. Do you want to have some breakfast?"

"Now you know I'm down to grub any day," she said, rubbing her stomach.

London walked over to Paris, giving her a hug and a kiss. Then she took a seat next to her. She saw the hurt in her sister's eyes, and it hurt her as well.

"So no phone call from Kalisha?" London asked.

Paris shook her head no, while swallowing two Advil. She talked to London about the conversation her and Bryce had about marriage and seeing a family therapist. They both finished up breakfast, and made their way to the backyard, stretching out on the huge spacious patio area. They carried on about everything that had transpired, from their mother's death. On up to what was going on at the moment, they stayed out on the patio talking for so long. They even talked about how April and London met London notice it was now 5:45pm when she picked up her Apple Phone. London needed to tell Paris something that was on her mind, but didn't know how to come about it. She was afraid of her sister getting upset and flipping out on her, but she felt in her heart that something needed to be said. up. However, I don't

"Paris. I hope you don't get mad at me, but I feel the need to bring this to your attention. Now I know what Bryce's mother did to our mother, and yes that was real messed think it's right for you to snap at Bryce about his mother. At the end of the day he is going to be there for her, and I don't want you and Bryce's relationship to go sour because of that. I still deal with that till this day about our mother, and how everything went down afterwards. Paris I even had to find it in my heart to forgive my Aunt B for taking me away from you, and then lying to me. I can't make her suffer, anymore, hell she is in prison. She is already being dealt with. Although this is different from Gloria being responsible for mom's death, but Paris please try not to take your anger out on Bryce when it comes to his mother. He is a damn good man, and I would hate to see you push him away. Maybe the family therapist is a good idea for you all, and me too. We all should come together and pull through this. So much shit has happened to us, and we didn't ask for it. All I'm saying is don't push Bryce away. He loves you so much. Just let him keep being there for his mother, whether if you and Gloria ever speak to each other or not." London let out a sigh, waiting for her sister to flip out on her. To her surprise she didn't. Paris sat there and listened to what her younger sister had to say.

"Yeah that's why we plan to talk to a family therapist before we get married." Paris replied.

"Oh My! So you guys are going to get married!" London jumped up for joy, happy as she could be.

"Girl stops it!" Paris playfully kicked at London.

"Okay! So let's talk about you and April! All I wanna know is WHEN, WHERE, WHY, and How!" They both laughed.

"Well, I met April while she was working for the Real Estate Company; I got my house from. I thought she was very attractive, and I really didn't do too well in relationships with guys. So we hung out a couple of times as friends, then it grew into something serious with us. When Bryce mentioned that he needed an assistant, I remember April saying she needed to look for another job because the Real Estate Company is going to be closing. So that's how she started working for Bryce, and this whole time you thought she wanted your man." London started to tease Paris, laughing at her.

"Well Sis, you happy, then I'm happy. That's all that matters. I love you no matter what." Paris said giving her a hug and a kiss.

The sky was starting to turn dark gray, notifying the City Houston was about to receive a hell of a storm. Paris and London make their way in the house, just as it started to thunder real loud unexpectedly, causing the two of them to jump and scream. Bryce walking out of his study laughing at them, and before you knows it. It started raining like cats and dogs.

"Girl Texas got some bipolar ass weather; damn it was just hot as hell a second ago!" London blurted out, walking into the kitchen.

Paris walks over to Bryce, placing a kiss on his lips. His arms around her waist.

"So when are we going to have a visit with Dr. Angela Jackson? Paris asked kissing him again. Bryce smiled. He was so happy that she wanted to make things with them.

"I will call her first thing in the morning." he replied still holding her.

"Baby, call April and make sure her and the kids are okay."

"Will do sweetie." Bryce replied walking into his study.

To Paris' surprise there was a knock at the door, then the doorbell rings.

"Now who in the hell decided to come over here in this damn weather!" London shouted, walking to the door, with a hand full of grapes.

London opened the door, dropping the hand full of grapes; backing away in fear. She was so scared, she couldn't even scream. As she witness the tall bald headed guy, holding Kalisha by the arm. With a gun pointing directly at her. She also took noticed of the little teen girl who was with them.

"Close your mouth and move the hell out of the way!" Clint barked at her.

Clint made his way into the house, shutting the door behind him with his foot. He ordered his daughter to go and sit down on the couch, as she was crying. Then he jacked Kalisha up and threw her onto the living room floor, like she was a rag doll.

"What the fuck?" Paris yelled running to Kalisha's side.

"OH MY GOD! Kalisha! Are you okay?" Paris and London were now on the floor with Kalisha, they barley even notice Clint standing over them with a gun.

"Okay, ladies! Get your asses up and go over to the couch next to my daughter!" he yelled, still pointing the gun at the three of them.

"What the hell do you want? Why are you doing this?" Paris yelled as she held Kalisha in her arms, crying.

"Well I'm about to explain this, after you all shut the fuck up! Stop all of that damn crying! Oh and you are gonna need those tears for later. After I'm done." Clint yelled in a deep tone. Pointing at Paris.

Bryce's walks in, Clint immediately turns around, pointing the gun at him.

"Whoa! What the hell?" Bryce throws his hands up in the air.

"Yeah, man! Get over there and sit your ass down with the ladies." Clint told Bryce.

Bryce walked over to the couch slowly, with his hands up in the air. Not taking his eyes off of Clint. Bryce saw Kalisha sitting on the couch in between Paris and London. Then he turned his focus back to Clint.

"Say, man! What's the problem? Whatever you want, you can have it, just don't hurt them." Bryce was trying to reason with Clint.

"Look, if I really wanted to hurt somebody, then she would be dead." He stated pointing at Kalisha, as she placed her face into her hands, still crying, wishing she was dead right about now. She knew that all of her skeleton bones were about to fall out of the closet, no doubt. Paris, London, and Bryce were all sitting looking confused as hell. They did not have not a clue of what was going on, none of this was making any sense at all. They could not understand how was it that Kalisha was missing, and then she ends up in Houston. Being held at gun point with this crazy man; at Paris' and Bryce's house. Even though Paris was happy to see that her best friend was still alive, but she really needed some answers about what the hell was really going on. Clint pulls the foot stool in the middle of the living room, making eye contact with everyone. Including his daughter who was sitting there crying her eyes out.

"Why don't you let the little girl go in the kids room, she is scared to death." Bryce asked Clint.

"No! She needs to hear everything that I'm about to say. I'm not here to hurt anybody, so please don't try any funny shit," Clint replied.

Kalisha cried even more, not wanting to look up at anybody. She knew that everything was about to come out, about what she did in her past. Clint cleared his throat, as if he was about to give a very important speech.

"Well! I'm here with Kalisha today because she refused to assist me with some financial difficulties. Now Paris, I understand that she is your best friend. Well so you think.

However she is really not your friend, she is a heartless whoring bitch. There's a lot that you have been left in a dark about, and I am here to shine that light for you, about your so called best friend. I hope you all are buckled up for safety, because this is about to be one hell of a ride."

Clint walked over to Kalisha, pulling her up by the arm. Making her sit on the other couch. Then he turned to his daughter.

"Brandy baby, come over here and sit with her."

The little girl did as she was told, taking a seat next to Kalisha. Then Clint jerked Kalisha by both arms, making her hug his daughter Brandy.

"Hold her! And you better not let go." He yelled pointing the gun at Kalisha's head. Kalisha held the little girl tight as she could, crying up a storm. While the child begged her father to stop, and let everything go.

By this time Paris, Bryce, and London were all wearing the look of confusion on their faces. They could not figure out what in the hell was going on, and who was this man who kidnapped Paris, and why did he bring her to Houston with this little girl who was his daughter. For some reason Paris and London wasn't crying anymore, they knew this guy was here for a purpose, but could not figure out why. Then Clint went back over to his seat, facing everyone to release the load off of his chest. Looking straight at Kalisha, he started to speak calmly.

"Now Kalisha. Could you please tell your best friend Paris, who is this child that you are holding? I think Paris would really appreciate hearing the news from you. I mean. You're her best friend. Right?" Clint snickered.

Kalisha shook her head no, with more tears.

Paris was growing very frustrated and impatient with the whole thing, and was about to lose it. "Well, somebody need start talking, because I'm really getting pissed off. Tell me what's going on!" Paris yelled. Kalisha looked down to the floor, not able to look at anyone. Still holding the child in her arms. Trying to speak without crying.

"Paris I know that you may hate me after this, but this is my child. After she was born I gave her away to a couple who was having trouble conceiving, which is him and his wife." Kalisha struggled to speak.

Paris and everyone else accept for Clint, sat with their mouths hanging wide open. At lost for words, completely speechless. All eyes now on Kalisha, as the light shine on her, waiting for each skeleton bone to fall out of the closet. One by one. Clint is now pissed, because Kalisha is not telling the whole story.

"So is that it? Is that all you have to say?" Clint standing to his feet, as Kalisha sat silent.

"Okay Paris! Since your friend here wants to act like she got amnesia, fuck it then. I will tell you the story." Clint flops back down onto the footrest, giving Kalisha a 'I hate you' look.

"Look, it's like this – My wife, Cynthia, and I wanted a child more than anything in this world. Cynthia only had one ovary, because of ovarian cancer, so it wasn't possible for us to have kids. We tried adoption agencies and we still had no luck with that – they denied us because of my wife's health issues. One day, my job at the water company sent me and my partner to deliver over at Frost Real Estate. This older guy – one of the owners by the name of Bradshaw Frost – was standing by when my partner and I unloaded the truck. He overheard me venting to my partner about me and Cynthia having trouble adopting a baby. When we were done unloading the water, Mr. Frost called me into his office. He told me he overheard me talking about our situation and mentioned that his son had messed around and got his fiancé's best friend pregnant, and that he needed help cleaning up his son's mess. However, I didn't see it as a mess; I saw it as a beautiful blessing for me and my wife. Bradshaw invited Cynthia and I over to his home in Westlake, so we could meet his son Bradley Frost. After sitting down for dinner, we had a very long discussion about Bradley and Kalisha's situation. A week later Cynthia and I took Kalisha into our home, when she was three months pregnant. Bradley talked her into transferring to Temple College, since we lived in Killeen. Bradley paid for her stay at our home. Once we found out that Kalisha was having a girl, Bradley sent all kinds of gift cards that equaled up to thousands of dollars so Cynthia could fix up the nursery. After Brandy was born and Kalisha healed up, she packed up, ready to go back to Austin. I don't even think she kissed Brandy goodbye. We all made an agreement that we would keep in contact for the sake of Brandy, and that if anything was to happen to me or my wife, Brandy would be taken care of by Bradley or Kalisha. Well, four months ago before my wife passed away, we were having financial problems. The medicine that Cynthia needed was so expensive and all the bills were on me. I was really having a hard time handling everything by myself; there were times when I couldn't even buy Brandy nice school clothes to wear. Hell, we didn't even know where our next meal was gonna come from sometime. At one point my back was completely against the wall, I had nobody to turn to – no family, no friends, no nothing. I picked up the phone to call Kalisha, and told her about everything that was going on. She hung up on me, and changed her number. I inbox her on Facebook, she blocked me. After a little time passed by, out of the blue, Bradley called me to check on Brandy. I shared with him about everything that was going on, and how cold Kalisha was acting. Then that's when he gave me the idea of going to Austin, so I could track Kalisha down. Sure she gave me $5,000 to go away, but when she spoke to me so coldly, telling me not to ever contact her again and that she didn't give a damn about Brandy – that's when I started to harass her by showing up to her job, and her daughter's soccer games. That's when I realized how heartless she was, and that she really didn't care about nobody but herself. I don't even know how her husband married her selfish ass. Not to mention, her last day in Killeen, my wife asked her just out of curiosity why she didn't choose get an abortion, and then she informed my wife on the real deal. She told her that she was hoping that if she held on to the baby, that one day Bradley would leave you to be with her. That's why she didn't have the abortion. So I figured I'd snatch her ass up and bring her here to Houston to expose all of her bullshit, since she wants to act like that. She thinks I dragged her up here to get money from you, but really I'm fine with the $5,000 she gave me. It's just how she went about everything, with her heartless and selfish ways. She really needs to understand that you can't just do people any kind of way, and expect to get through life untouchable. So that's why we are here today, I'm not here to hurt anybody. Just only to expose the truth."

By the time Clint was finished with his long and shocking speech, the room was completely silent. Everyone sat on the couch with blank stares, as if they just watched a movie with a cliff hanger at the end. Bryce and London glanced over at Paris, to see her reaction. She was crying silent tears. Kalisha was too, with Brandy still in her arms. Then three different text alerts caught everyone off guard, still speechless from the shocking news. Bryce, Paris, and London all three grab their phones, to open the forward text that was sent to the three of them. From Jermaine. London must have opened hers first because she was the first to gasp, then Paris and Bryce gasped. Revealing the picture that Jermaine found in Kalisha's safe. A picture of Kalisha lying in a hospital bed, holding a baby girl wrapped up in a pink blanket. With Bradley in the picture by her side. They all three give Kalisha the nastiest look ever. Paris blood was definitely boiling, her body quivered with rage. Bryce knew what this meant, he knew Paris very well. But Brandy managed to speak first.

"No matter what you will always be my daddy and I love you. Now can we please go home?" Brandy gently pulled away from Kalisha and joined Clint by the couch.

That gave Paris the opportunity to assault Kalisha as swiftly as she could. She flew over to where Clint was, grabbing his gun and pointing it directly at Kalisha. In a flash, she had snatched up a handful of the woman's hair, pressing the gun into the side of her head, as hard as she could. Bryce ran over to stop her, but he was no help.

"You bitch," Paris screamed in her face. "I should kill your ass right here, right now." Kalisha sobbed pitifully.

"Paris, no, please put the gun down," Bryce begged. "Honey it's not worth it." He tried to carefully ease his way over to take the gun, but Paris ignored him.

"You triflin' ass bitch," she cried. "You were my best friend – my sister. You were there when I lost my mother. We've been through everything together! So after I found out that I was pregnant with B.J and moved out of your mother's house, that's why you had a nasty attitude when I tried to come give you a hug? You got up and went back into the house. Then you disappeared for six months. Damn, now it's all coming together. I guess it's true then."

"Paris, it's not worth it, sis please don't!" London whispered.

Bryce rubbed her shoulder gently, sliding his hand down her arm toward the gun. "Baby please thinks about our family – the kids. She's not worth it honey. Come on, please Paris, give me the gun. Don't hurt our children, don't break their hearts. Your mother is looking down at you. Baby don't do it."

"Baby please just give me the gun." Bryce speaks into her ear.

Paris finally let go, and give the gun to Bryce. Once she and Kalisha both stood to their feet. Paris immediately stole off on Kalisha, giving her a good blow to the side of her jaw. Kalisha's body spins around, dropping to the floor. Paris runs over to her, serving her a good kick to the side of her waist. Causing Kalisha to roll over on her backside, Paris jumps on top of her, punching her everywhere she could. All kinds of built up anger was making its way out of Paris, and Kalisha was receiving it left and right. Once Bryce felt like it was enough, he grabs Paris, and bear hugs her into a corner. Paris continues to breath heavy, sweating up a storm. Still trying to get back over to Kalisha who was still lying on the floor.

"Now don't think that ass whooping was because of Bradley's punk ass! That was for the disrespect of our friendship! Bitch how could you!" She yells out to Kalisha, with Bryce pulling her away.

Bryce keeps a tight bear hug grip around Paris's body, making sure she doesn't get away. She already had done enough damage to Kalisha. Her face seems to be swollen really bad, possibility of her nose being broken. Along with a busted lip, and other facial bruising. Bryce instructed London to stay locked in his study with Paris, while he called her father Jamaican George. George arrived within ten minutes. He took Kalisha to the emergency room, and made her tell the doctor and nurses, that she got jumped by a group of females in Fifth Ward. She did as she was told. After her release from the hospital, George drove her back to Austin, and instructed her to inform the police that she had ran off with an old friend, and that she was not kidnapped. So Clint would not get charged with anything, Brandy really needed her father. Yes he was wrong for kidnapping Kalisha, but after hearing him out, and how cold Kalisha treated him when he asked her for help. George made sure that he prepared a long drawn out lie for Kalisha to tell the hospital and the police. Even though the whole situation was messed up with what Kalisha did to Paris?

George being the kind heart person that he is, he made sure that she made it back home safe. He was still looking at the fact that Kalisha was still somebody's daughter, and he would want someone to look out for Paris or even London, if they were ever in that type of predicament.

Chapter Sixteen

Days, weeks, and even a month had passed on by. Ever since the unpleasant pop up from Kalisha and Clint, Paris wasn't herself at all; in fact, she had gotten worse. She stayed locked up in her room for days at a time, leaving the kids to take care of themselves. It would take the twins and Brielle to knock on her door crying in order for her to come out. Then she would ease her way back in her room, locking the door, just to crawl back in bed. She was hurting mentally, and emotionally. She slipped into a deep depression, and was in need of some serious help. Prayer was really the first thing that she needed.

Bryce walked in the house, walking into the family room. Noticing that the twins had bags of chips, and cookies all over the place. Then he walked into the kitchen, to see that frozen pizza boxes were everywhere. Paris hadn't got up to cook, and clearly the kids been eating all types of junk food. He stormed straight to the bedroom, snatching the covers off of Paris and pulling the bedroom curtains back, allowing the sun to sit right on top of her face.

"What the hell are you doing?" she yelled at him, trying to snatch the covers back.

"Paris I'm not playing with you! Get your ass up now!" Bryce barked at her. Which was something rare. Nowadays he never even raised an eyebrow at Paris, even when she would act out of order.

"What is it, Bryce!"

"I need for you to get your shit together, get your ass out of bed. Go in there and be a mother to your damn children. I'm serious Paris! I know everything that happened is real fucked up, that's why I want you to get some help. Paris we can go through this together, I can't stand to see you like this." Bryce pleaded with her, as he sat on the side of the bed next to her.

"I just want to be left the hell alone!"

"Okay Paris. It's like this, if you don't get any help. Then I'm leaving you, and I'm taking the kids with me. All four of them."

Paris stood up, facing Bryce.

"You not taking all four of nothing, in case you forgot only the twins belong to you, and you are not taking them either."

"Well, B.J and Brielle are still my niece and nephew, in case you forgot, and yes I will still take them away."

Paris blood was now boiling; she couldn't speak not one word. She became furious, nearly foaming out of the mouth. Bryce had really struck a nerve, she was about to lose it and let him have it. Bryce took note of her facial expression, making an attempt to step back away from her. He had not a clue of what was going on inside of her head at all, and was trying to get the hell away from her.

"You son of a bitch!"

Paris screamed trying to whack him with the lamp, she grabbed from the night stand. Bryce ducked, making his way to the door as fast as he could.

"Your family is the one who ruined my life, and now you talking about taking my kids away! You bastard!"

She took one more swing at him. This time he caught the lamp, by snatching it out of her hand. Grabbing her, throwing her onto the floor. Causing her to hit her head on the dresser. Bryce standing over her as she lay there crying, anger is now written all over his face. His breathing becomes heavier and heavier, as he stares at her.

"That's it! I'm gone, and you are right. I can't take B.J and Brielle with me, but I can sure as hell take my twins. If you really love your children, you should send them to your sister's house or your dad's house so you can get some help. However I'm taking the twins, and if you get up off that floor acting crazy, I will choke the living shit out of you."

Paris continued to lie there, sobbing and crying. For her that was unexpected and shocking. Bryce had never laid a hand on her, or talked to her so cold. It somewhat scared her to see Bryce react in such a way. Bryce pulled out two black duffle bags, and filling them both up with clothes. Stepping over Paris back and forth like she wasn't even there and he had no idea how much that was killing her. After he was done he went into the twins' room, and packed their bags as well. Paris still hadn't gotten up off the floor; she could overhear Bryce talking to the kids.

"Why are you leaving? Why do the twins get to go? Can B.J and I go with you?" She could hear Brielle in the hallway crying, which made her cry even more.

"Sweetheart. Listen you know I love you very much, you and your brother. Right now mommy is not well, and I have to go get mommy some help. Your Auntie and Papa will be here shortly, I just called them to come over." Bryce tried to explain to Brielle the best way he could, without breaking down.

Paris could hear Bryce's footsteps getting closer to the bedroom door, as she still lay there in the same position.

"Hey, you need to get up, the twins want to give you hugs and kisses goodbye. Go in the bathroom and wash your face, at least brush your hair into a ponytail or something. I don't want the kids to see you looking a hot mess. So get up." He spoke so cold to her, standing in the doorway.

She got up, did as she was told. Still crying with bloodshot red eyes, grabbing a pair of gray jogging pants, and a white shirt to put on. After receiving hugs and kisses from the twins, Bryce sent them out of the room, telling them to wait at the front door. He turned to Paris, giving her a nasty look, and shaking his head. Walking out with his bags, as Paris tries to talk.

"Bryce where are you and the kids going to be staying?" She cries out to him, but he ignores her, and keeps on walking.

After London came over to pick up Brielle and B.J, she informed Paris that she was going to be looking out for her Group Home Service, and make sure everything was running smoothly. Once Paris was left alone in that big giant two story house, all by herself with no one by her side. That's when it hit her. She finally realized that if she didn't get help, she was going to be all alone.

Bryce tossed and turned for about three days now, not being able to sleep. He missed Paris so much, to where it hurt him. Although he was just around the corner from her, at her father's house. Staying in his guest bedroom, but he refused to call her and tell her that. He really wanted her to feel it; of what was it like for him not to be there. Not just him, but the kids to where gone also. Once Bryce got the twins off to school, he sent Paris a text message. Letting her know that Dr. Angela Jackson was going to be over to see her, he had spoken with Dr. Jackson while he was getting the twins ready for school. He wanted so bad to run back home to Paris, and make passionate love to her, but he was to stand his ground. He wanted things to be right between the two of them so bad, he loved her more than anything in this world. Walking into his office, reaching to open the bottom drawer. He pulled out the tumor size diamond ring, flopped in his office chair. Staring at it, he wanted that diamond on Paris's finger so bad. He just felt that it wasn't the right time at this moment.

Dr. Jackson sat with Paris out in the patio area of the home for about two and a half hours, as Paris finally opened up about everything that has taking place in her life, up until now at that very moment. Dr. Jackson was very sweet and soft spoken, and a very spiritual person. With long sandy red hair, and a red apple colored skin tone, with freckles. She wasn't just a family therapist; she was also a woman of God.

"Paris. The first thing we must do is pray, and give it all to God. You may not want to hear this, but you also have to forgive everyone who has hurt you. It's not good to carry grudges. You are gonna have to forgive your ex-husband, your ex mother in-law, and your ex father in-law may he rest in peace. Then you are gonna have to pray to God every single day, that he can bring you through all of this. Now, it will not happen overnight, but you have got to keep him close to you. He will not put too much on you that you cannot handle, take it one day at a time. Now, I have to get back over to the office. I would like for us to meet again next week, but before I go, we must pray."

Soon, Dr. Jackson was gone. Paris walked over to the kitchen calendar, noticing that it was Friday. That's when she decided to get up early the next Saturday morning, and take her a little road trip.

Paris felt somewhat nervous, as she pulled up into Holliday Unit Prison. In Huntsville, Texas. A part of her wanted to turn back around, get in her car, and drive back to Houston. She chose not to do so; she already had come too far. Not to mention it was a heavy load that she really needed to get off of her chest, this was the start of her healing process. Once she was patted down by a female guard, she was instructed to take a seat at the white table in the back corner of the visiting room. She was kind of glad to be way in the back, just in case she had to say a few harsh words. The guards and everyone might not hear her. The palms of her hands started to sweat, her right leg shook uncontrollably. She scanned the visiting room for a few seconds, noticing a Spanish lady with two small toddlers walking in. Her heart instantly went out to the lady; she remembered how it was dragging B.J and Brielle to see Bradley when he first got locked up. Ten minutes after waiting here he comes walking out. She hasn't seen him in over nine years, and was surprised at his appearance. Very tall with thick broad shoulders, thick arms, and a pair of reading glasses. Wearing all white, with white sneakers, still handsome as ever. The inmate was in complete shock himself, Paris was the last person that he was expecting a visit from. He gave a slight grin, so amazed at how beautiful she was after all these years.

"Hello, Paris Frost. Oh, I'm sorry... did you go back to Paris Scott? Damn, it's been a long time."

"Hello Bradley." Paris rolled her eyes.

"Well, damn can I get a hug?" Bradley asked still standing, with his arms open. Once he saw the scowl on Paris' face, he took a seat. But he held the same grin on his face, looking like an older version of BJ; he really didn't age all that must but a couple of grey hairs were visible at the tip of his hairline.

"Look Bradley I'm not here to have no heart to heart conversation with you, and honestly it's taking everything in me to not punch you dead in your face. So shut up and hear me out."

"Okay Paris. What brings you here after nine years? And where are my kids? " He said taking a deep breath, clasping his hands together and staring her straight in the eye.

"Bradley, I just want to know why? Why did you hurt me? Why did you make my life a living hell? Why did you do the things that you did? What did I do to deserve it?"

Bradley stared at her for a couple of seconds, in silent without a blink. Then he spoke.

"So you wait over nine years to ask me this shit, after you sent me divorce papers. This is really some ass backwards shit; you came all the way out here to ask me that."

Paris was already growing sick in the stomach, within five minutes of the visit. She could not believe after all these years he was still arrogant as hell. She was really trying so hard not to curse him out. She sat for a little bit, trying to collect her thoughts and words.

"Bradley you have no idea how much you have fucked my life up. I can't even look at B.J cause when I do, all I see you. I even have nightmares about you from time to time. It screws with my head every time Bradley. Not only that – I found out about you and Kalisha's secret child. How could you do that? She was my best friend. Out of all the females in Austin, you just had to mess with my best friend." Paris did her best to fight back tears.

"Paris, if I could go back and change the past I would, but I can't." Bradley spoke casually, like always while addressing his wrong doings.

"Why the hell I don't believe you!" Paris hissed at him.

"Look I do have a lot of regrets, but it's not shit I can do about it now. So why you here asking me all these damn questions? Where are my damn kids? And why the hell you stop bringing them to see me? Regardless of whatever went on between us, you had no right to take my kids away from me. Then Bryce was bringing B.J for a little bit, and then he stopped. I shouldn't have never had to go through my brother to see my kids, and as for that bastard I got a few words for him when I get out." He barked at her from across the table.

Paris cleared her throat, sitting up straight, making eye contact. Ready to end her visit with Bradley, and she had only been in there for fifteen minutes. That's how bad he was pissing her off, and she was not able to take another minute of it, without exploding on him.

"Bradley you have never allowed me to own my own feelings, and express how you made me feel. Even though it was years ago, but at the same time you need to be aware of all the horrible things you have done, and how it's affected my life right now today as we speak. After all of the shit you have put me through, I have got to forgive you and move on in life. I even have to forgive your mother and your father. So I'm here to say that I forgive you, and I pray that you have asked God to forgive you for all of your wrongs." Paris wiped the tears from her eyes.

"Look, Paris. I know a lot of shit was fucked up, but you don't understand – I was introduced to that lifestyle at an early age. All I cared about was making money, that's how my father mold me into a younger version of him. As for your friend Kalisha – she wasn't nothing but a hoe. I was gonna make her get an abortion but she purposely waited to tell me after she was four months pregnant. Then that's when you found out that you were pregnant with B.J. So that's why I hurried up and married you so you could move out of Kalisha's mom's house. She was secretly jealous of you, she saw the lifestyle that you were about to be living. The day you were moving out of her mother's house, she called me crying. Begging me to make you have an abortion."

Paris was really in even more shock, listening to everything that Bradley had just put out on the table, she couldn't believe that she never saw any signs of Kalisha and Bradley's secret affair. She felt so stupid, thinking back to the day when she went over to try and hug Kalisha goodbye. The day she was moving, and how Kalisha got up and went into the house without saying anything. The whole time she though that her best friend was sad, because she didn't want her to leave. Meanwhile, the whole time, she was jealous because Paris pregnant with Bradley's baby, and Bradley wanted to marry her instead.

"Boy, I tell you... the two of you are some low down dirty ass dogs, but you know what – God's gonna handle that. I want you to think about something, or should I say someone. Keep in mind that you have a daughter, well two daughters at that. How would you feel if a man treated them the way you treated me?"

Bradley sat in silence for a few seconds, with his lips half way turned up. His whole demeanor and body language was really pissing Paris off, and she knew by then that it was time for her to go.

"So you don't have anything to say?" Paris asked with a frown.

"Yeah as a matter fact I do. The next time you come down here, bring my kids. Also, I'm gonna need the keys to the storage unit so I can get my furniture set and those teddy bears back." He gazed at Paris unblinking.

Paris bit her bottom lip and stood up. She wanted so bad to slap him, but she knew she couldn't. After taking a couple of deep breaths, she finally spoke. "Goodbye, Bradley. I'll be praying for you."

"It's cool, Paris. Just know that I won't be in here forever, we shall see each other again. I promise you that, honey." A devilish smiled appeared on his face.

Paris stormed off as fast as she could, heading for the front desk where the middle aged correctional officer was sitting.

"Hello Ma'am, I need to sign out." Paris approached the desk.

"Wow! That was a short visit." The female officer stated, when noticing the in and out time of thirty minutes Paris signed for.

"Yes, Ma'am. I really didn't have much to say that required a two hour visit."

After the visit Paris had with Bradley, she knew that she was definitely gonna have to give Dr. Angela Jackson a call for another session. She hopped in her Escalade, making her way back to Houston. Then she turned on the radio and allowed The Isley Brothers to sooth her nerves.

Chapter Seventeen

George's heart instantly smiled, not taking his eyes off of Paris. Dressed in her all white sleeveless gown, with a white Lily Flower on the side of her head, stuck into her pin up curls. She reminded him of Billie Holiday. She was so beautiful, and George tried his best to keep from crying.

"Are you ready, Baby Girl?" He asked, locking arms with her, with a smile. They strutting down the beautiful Hawaiian beach. He never thought in a million years, that he would get a chance to give his daughter away on her wedding day. This was the day that he lived for. Paris was all smiles herself, as she and her father walked down to Bryce's and the Hawaiian Pastor's direction. Bryce looked so good dressed in his all white silk shirt sleeve shirt, and white slacks. Not taking his eyes off of his bride. Brielle and the twins stood on the side, dressed in all white as well, and B.J stood next to Bryce as his best man. London on the other side as the Maid of Honor. Once Paris and her father approached everyone, Bryce took Paris by both hands, looking over at George.

"Now you keep taking care of my baby girl," George said to Bryce as he patted him on the back, with a huge smile.

Bryce was damn near in tears. He loved Paris so much, he was so happy that this day had finally arrived. After everything they had gone through, Bryce let it be known to Paris that he wanted marriage. He felt like they were so blessed, that they should do the right thing. After Paris completed her session with Dr. Angela Jackson, she started to have more of a better understanding about things. She and Bryce decided to fly out to Hawaii, with just their family, and get married on the beautiful Maui Beach. Once their vows were exchanged, and Bryce kissed his bride. Everyone clapped with all smiles, and joy.

London approached Paris as she took sips of her Champagne, at the small dinner gathering they had at their hotel. She was so happy that her big sister made the right decision to marry Bryce.

"Sis, words can't explain how happy I am for the two of you. He loves you so much." London smiled from ear to ear.

"Thanks, honey." Paris leaned in, kissing her on the forehead.

"So are you guys gonna have any more kids?" London asked as she giggled.

"Girl, hell no! Brielle and the twins keep me busy enough." They both burst into laughter.

Dance With My Father, by Luther Vandross, flowed through the air, and Paris and George grinned at one another.

"Can I have this dance?" he asked.

"Of course, Daddy." Paris smiled.

"I'm so grateful that God has allowed me to be here with you, especially on this beautiful day of yours. You look so much like your mother; I know that she is looking down, smiling at you."

A tear fell from Paris's eye, as she imagined her mother being there with her on her special day. She knew that her mother would have been all smiles. As Paris and George continued on with their father and daughter dance, she glanced over at B.J and Bryce. As they carried on a deep conversation with each other at the dinner table, then she noticed the two of them slapping fives, and handshakes with each other. She was so blessed to have a normal relationship with her son again and now a beautiful marriage with Bryce. She was also very happy that B.J didn't look at her any different, for being with his Uncle Bryce who was also now his stepfather. She wasn't sure if Brielle fully understood everything, with the history and all. However B.J had a good understanding, and he also knew how bad his father Bradley hurt his mother Paris. He looked passed everything else, all he saw and all he cared about, was that his mother was happy. Paris thought that one day when Brielle and the twins got a little older, she would sit down and explain everything to them. It's was one thing that she didn't want to do, and that was keep anything away from none of her kids. She remembered how it made her and London feel, when they discovered all the hurtful skeleton bones that came falling out of the closet. Years after their mother Corina passed away, she never wanted her kids to experience that type of hurt.

Make It Last Forever by Keith Sweat, made its way through the speakers. George already knew what time it was, so he signaled for Bryce to come over and have his dance with Paris. Once he made his way, he smiled at George.

"May I cut in, Mr. Scott?"

"Say Man! It's okay to call me Dad or Pops." George playfully nudged at Bryce, as they both laughed.

George walked over to B.J, leaving Paris and Bryce to dance together. Bryce stared deeply into her set of hazels, not able to stop smiling. She truly had his heart, he loved her so much.

"Paris I love you so much, I can't imagine life without you baby. You and the kids are my everything." Bryce stated still not taking his eyes off of her, as they slow danced.

"Bryce besides the kids, you are the best thing that God has blessed me with. I'm so glad that I didn't lose you baby, you're my world, and I love you so much," she replied back.

Neither one of them wanted the night to end; it was such a beautiful night, and a very special day for the both of them. They both fell in love all over again.

After the dinner gathering, Paris and Bryce made their way back to their hotel suite. The kids, London, and George flew back to Houston so Paris and Bryce could have a couple of days alone in Hawaii. They really needed it. Once Paris and Bryce kissed everyone goodbye, sending them off to the airport by the car service company. Paris went into her purse for a stick of gum, but noticed the blue light on her phone flashing. She started ignore it, but then decided not to. Opening the screen to her phone to see that she had five new messages, and eight missed calls. She immediately walked inside the hotel lobby to check her messages, hoping and praying that everything was okay at her group homes.

First Message: "Paris! This is Jermaine. I didn't know who else to call, but Kalisha swallowed a bottle of pills, and had to be rushed to the hospital. She flipped out when I told her that I filed for a divorce, and she tried to kill herself. Paris please call me back as soon as you get this message."

Paris didn't bother to check the other four messages, she ran as fast as she could out of the hotel lobby, and outside right into Bryce's arms as he was making his way back in. Breathing heavy, as her forehead formed sweat beads.

"Baby what's wrong?" Bryce asked with a scared look on his face.

"Kalisha is in the hospital, she tried to kill herself. I think we should fly out to Austin for Jermaine and Corina." Paris tried her best to fight back tears, but wasn't able to. Even with everything coming to the light about Kalisha and Bradley's secret child, she still wanted to be there for Jermaine and Corina. Not to mention Dr. Angela Jackson had really been working with Paris on forgiveness, and that particular session could not have taken place at a better time. She was still very hurt about everything, but still felt the need to go be by Jermaine's side.

The very next day Paris and Bryce landed at Austin Bergstrom Airport. After picking up the rental, they made their way straight to Avery Ranch, as Paris stared so hard out of the car window. Noticing how much her hometown Austin had grown over nine years, even mid-day traffic had increased. She felt somewhat awkward being back in Austin, where all the memories she left behind. Pulling into Avery Ranch Subdivision, the first thing that popped into Paris's head was when she and Bryce first made love, when he had his house in Avery Ranch before they moved to Houston. After turning the car ignition off, Bryce reaches over taking Paris by her hand.

"Honey, are you going to be okay?" He asked with concern.

She shook her head yes in silence, opening up the car door to get out. She really didn't know what to expect as they walked up to the door, ringing the doorbell. Once Jermaine opened the door, he and Bryce immediately embraced each other. Then Jermaine did the same with Paris, as tears started to roll down her face.

"Where is Corina? Is she okay?" Paris asked.

"Yes she is fine; she is in her room taking a nap. You guys come on in and get comfortable; I know the two of you had a very long flight." Jermaine replied, shutting the front door.

Paris scanned the spacious well decorated living room, and then her eyes glanced over at the 8x10 photo sitting on top of the fireplace. She noticed it was a picture of her and Kalisha, from there teen years. When they went to a UGK concert during the summer of 1997, in Corpus Christi. A slight grin appeared on her face, but more tears also made their way down her face.

"You guys can put your things in the guest bedroom upstairs, I ordered Chinese for dinner, if that's okay." Jermaine stated as he took Paris' bags.

"Sure Jermaine that's cool. You really didn't have to do that, I mean we came here to be by you and Corina's side. With everything that you are going through, we are not expecting you cater to us." Bryce said to him.

Sitting at the dining room table, as everyone picked over their meal. Paris barely touched her Beef and Broccoli, which was one of her favorite Chinese Dishes. Bryce took notice of her demeanor, and became a little concern. He was worried about Paris slipping back into a deep depression again, considering she had not been out of therapy too long. Bryce cleared his throat, preparing to speak.

"So Jermaine, how are you holding up man? I know that this has really got to be hard on you and Corina."

"I'm okay. My heart is really hurting for my daughter, she is so sad about her mommy. I don't know how to explain everything to her about what's going on, the only thing that I can tell her is that mommy is sick, and she needs to get well. From the looks of things, I don't know if Kalisha is ever going to get well. Even though they pumped her stomach and all, but she is still not the same. It's like she is a zombie, she won't even talk." Out of nowhere Jermaine broke down.

Paris got up to stand by his side, taking him into her arms. As he continued to cry his heart out, nonstop. Bryce came along to stand on the other side of Jermaine, with his hand on his shoulder. Kalisha was still his wife, and he loved her very much. His heart ached over and over, from discovering Kalisha's secret, and now with her being in the hospital because of her trying to take her own life. He even thought to himself if he had made the mistake of filing for a divorce, he was starting to feel like all of this was his fault.

"Jermaine you have go to be strong for Corina, she needs you." Paris said to him, as she held him in her arms.

Early morning had arrived with the alarm clock going off at 7:30 am, in the guest room where Paris and Bryce slept in. Bryce reaches over to hit the snooze button, then taking his hand to feel for Paris on the other side of the bed. Only to notice that her side of the bed was empty. His body jumps up, noticing that Paris was sitting on the love seat. With her face buried into both of her hands, as she sobbed away.

"Baby! Are you okay?" Bryce ran to her side

"Bryce I don't think I'm ready to go up to the hospital, and see her just yet. I thought that I was ready, but I'm not baby. I can't do it right now." She cried even more.

Bryce held her even tighter in his arms.

"Paris, that is fine. You don't have to go; if you want you can just stay here with Corina. Jermaine and I will go, if that's what you want." He spoke so smooth and soft into her ear.

After Jermaine and Bryce left out to go visit Kalisha at the hospital, Paris washed the dishes from breakfast. Once she was finished, she made her way into the living room, joining Corina while she was watching one of her favorite shows on the Disney Channel.

"Hey Beautiful!" Paris flopped on the couch right next to her, as Cornia sat there in her pink pajama set, twirling the remote in her hand.

"Auntie Paris. Is mommy going to come back home?" Corina asked with sadness in her eyes.

Paris was stunned, and didn't know what to say. She took Corina in her arms, holding her tight. Placing a kiss on her forehead.

"Baby your mom is in one of the best hospitals, that's going to help her get well so she can come home. It may not be today or tomorrow, but just know that your mother loves you very much. God is going to see to it that she will be just fine." Paris did her best to explain to Corina.

Paris wanted to breakdown and cry; it really broke her heart to see Corina so sad. Being there with Corina also made her miss her kids, she wanted so bad to be lying on the couch with all four of them watching movies, and being silly. In order to try and take Corina's mind off of her mother, Paris decided to take her out to lunch for some pizza. It made Corina feel a little better. Once Paris and Corina arrived back to the house, she saw that Jermaine and Bryce made it back before she did. Walking into the house to find both Jermaine and Bryce, sitting on the couch, with blank stares along with sadness. That was Paris' cue to take Corina into her room, with one of her favorite Disney DVDs.

"Hi, Daddy! Auntie Paris took my out for pizza, and we went to play Putt-Putt Golf." Corina ran up to Jermaine, so excited and full of joy. Jumping into his lap.

"That's great sweetie. I'm glad you had fun with Auntie Paris" Jermaine replied back, as a tear feel from his eye, trying to force a smile. As he managed to not let Corina see him cry.

"Corina, Auntie Paris needs to talk to Daddy and Uncle Bryce. Let's grab a movie for you to watch in your room."

"Okay Auntie Paris!" Corina said in a happy cheerful voice, running to grab a movie from the rack.

Once Paris made her way back into the living room, she immediately took a seat right next to Bryce on the couch. Looking so scared and confused.

"Okay. What's going? How is Kalisha doing?" Paris asked with her eyes dotting back and forth from Jermaine to Bryce.

Jermaine wiped his eyes, trying his best to gather his words together.

"They transferred her to a mental hospital. Kalisha finally started talking, saying that she was gonna try to kill herself again."

"Are you serious?" Paris said with hurt in her eyes.

"Not only that! She just told me that Corina is not my daughter." Jermaine spoke with his forehead resting inside the palm of his hands.

"What did you just say?" Paris stood to her feet.

"Yeah! She figured since I filed for divorce, and I was leaving her. She thought that she should tell me this. Boy I tell you. That woman has hurt me in so many ways; I have been nothing but good to her. She can stay her ass in that damn mental hospital for all I care. That triflin bitch!" Jermaine screamed, as he jumped up.

Snatching the wedding picture of him and Kalisha from the living room table. Throwing it across the room, up against the wall. The glass shattering everywhere. Jermaine flopped back down onto the couch, and broke down as he cried his heart out. Bryce in silence, and Paris mouth wide open. At this point too many skeletons were making their way out of the closet; Paris was not able to take no more. She searched for words as her mind started to race a 100 mph. She could not believe that her best friend Kalisha was just down right dirty, and the messed up part about it. Paris never saw any type of signs about her being so deceitful. She walked over to Jermaine, sitting next to him still searching for words.

"Jermaine, I know that this is going to sound crazy and all. However, do you think Kalisha is just telling you this to hurt you? I mean sometimes us women will let our emotions get the best of us, to where we will say some messed up shit. Then end up regretting it. Also Jermaine, take into consideration that Kalisha is sick; she is really not herself at this point. So she just might be talking out the side of her head." Paris trying to reason with Jermaine.

"Paris I thought about that, but the fact that this has already crossed my mind when Corina was about two years old. I noticed that when she cries her eyes turn like a hazel green color, but when she is happy they go back to her normal light brown color. Neither one of us have colored eyes. Not to mention, Kalisha and I both have a wide nose, and full lips. Corina's nose is very small, and she has small thin lips. Oh and let's not get started on her red hair and freckles. Who in the hell has red hair and freckles in her family, or mines? No One! So whoever Corina's real father is he has to be either white or mixed with Irish or something. I know that I'm not the only one who noticed it."

After Jermaine made his statement with tears, Paris thought back to the day when she gave birth to the twins. She remembered that another doctor had to deliver her twins, because her doctor was not available that night. So she had to settle for Dr. Perry. A tall slender, red headed gentleman that was an Irish decent. Even though Paris was zoning in and out on the medications, but she took noticed to how Kalisha was all smiles and giggles that night. Whenever Dr. Perry left out the room, Kalisha would leave out also. Coming back a thirty minutes to an hour later, acting like she was floating on cloud nine. Paris noticed that Kalisha was acting weird that night, but didn't really pay it no mind. She took two deep breaths, still searching her words, and then she spoke.

"Jermaine. Listen, just know that Corina loves you very much, right now you are all that she has. Bryce and I are here for you guys also, but no matter what. You are Corina's father. I don't give a damn how red her hair is, or what color her eyes are. You are her father." Paris stated.

Too many days had gone by; Paris really needed to be at home with her kids. She missed them so much, it hurt her like hell. Right before saying their good byes, Bryce walked over to Jermaine. Embracing him, and he picked Corina up and gave her a big hug and a kiss.

"Uncle loves you, and you call me or your Auntie Paris whenever you want to come and visit. Okay." Bryce said to Corina, and then he went to place their bags in the trunk of the car.

Paris got up from the porch, making her way over to Jermaine and Corina. She felt so bad for leaving, she felt even worse for Corina. She remembered how she felt after losing her mom, even though Kalisha was still alive, but she wasn't herself at all anymore. So in a way Corina did lose her mother, and Paris knew exactly what that felt like.

"Come here Beautiful." Paris said to Corina.

Corina ran right into Paris's arms, with nothing but smiles.

"Listen Honey. I want you to know that I'm here for you, and if you ever want to call me, or even come to Houston to visit us. Auntie Paris is just a phone call away. I love you Baby Girl."

"I love you to Auntie Paris." Corina gave Paris a big kiss on her cheek.

"As for you, Mr. Man! You already know what to do if you need anything, Bryce and I are here for you and Corina, so don't ever feel like you are alone. We got you." Paris said to Jermaine as she gave him a hug.

"Thank you Paris. Make sure you call as soon as the two of you get home safe. Love you all."

Chapter Eighteen

Bryce was extremely nervous as he sat in the visitation room watching the clock on the gray brick wall. The night before he tossed and turned, unable to rest, knowing he'd be seeing his mother again after all this time. It really broke his heart, having to visit her in prison, and he didn't know how he was gonna be able to cope with that. A buzzing came through the speakers; it reminded him of when he was locked up. Then the door opened and a young officer entered, pushing an old lady in a wheelchair. He really didn't pay attention until the officer parked the white-haired lady right across from him.

The officer made a mistake. He had brought the old lady to the wrong table. "Uh, ma'am..." He began to flag the officer down, but hesitated, realizing he spoke too soon. Another look at the inmate told him that it was, in fact, his mother. He hardly recognized her. With all the wrinkles in her face, her mouth was twisted, and bags hung in rings under her eyes. She looked nothing like herself at all. The officer turned around with a quizzical brow. "Never mind..."

Gloria was only in her late forties, but the stroke, along with previous plastic surgery that she had, made her look as if she was in her seventies. The woman Bryce was looking at was the woman who practically lived in the salon, once upon a time. She would never leave the house without her hair and makeup on point. He fought back tears the best way he could, but this was all a huge shock to him.

"Hey, Mom. How are you doing?" Bryce got up to hug Gloria.

"I see my baby boy finally came to see me after all of these years." She replied back in a slurred speech.

"Mama I'm sorry for letting all of this time go by, I really don't know what to say."

"Aw Baby it's okay. Your letters and cards keeps me going, I miss you and your brother so much."

"I miss you to mom. How are you feeling, far as your health?"

"I'm holding up, sweetie."

Bryce held his head down for a couple of seconds, and then he looked back up at his mother.

"Are you able to receive the right medications that you need mom?"

"Yes Honey. Believe it or not, the nurses here are good at what they do." She replied back with a smile, and then she spoke again.

"Bryce. Honey I want to say that I am sorry for everything. Starting from the day you were born. I'm sorry that I have allowed Bradshaw to treat you so harsh throughout your childhood, and I'm sorry that he was the cause of you to serve time in prison. Especially for some shit that you weren't even a part of, I even hate that he introduced Bradley into that lifestyle. Me being wrapped up in money and other materialistic things, I was so blinded by a lot. The night I was gonna leave Bradshaw, when I found out that he killed Johnny Lopez; your real father. I should have still left him, but I was so worried about leaving behind the lavished lifestyle. I wasn't thinking what was best for my kids; I was being selfish and thinking about myself. Now look at me. I'm sitting here in prison for being responsible for the murder of his mistress Corina Scott. I know I can't change the past, but I have asked God to forgive me. I even pray that Paris will one day find it in her heart to forgive me, for having her mother killed."

When Bryce heard his mother mentioned Paris name, he shifted in his chair, looking away from his mother. Gloria noticed the change in his demeanor right off the back. Even though it had been close to ten years since she has seen her son, but she was still his mother, and she knew something was wrong but couldn't put her finger on it.

"Son, are you okay?" Gloria asked with a concern look on her face.

"Yes Mom. I'm fine." He replied back not looking at her.

"Okay if you say so son." Gloria chuckled a little. Then she continued on.

"I see you got a nice wedding band there on your finger, who is the lucky lady? She smiled at Bryce.

"Aw, Mom, it's a prayer ring." He lied.

Bryce wanted so bad to tell his mother the truth about him and Paris, but he was not able to bring himself to do so. He still hadn't even told her about the twins. He figured one day he would tell her, but today was just not gonna happen. They finished out their two hour visit, mostly talking about memories. As they snacked on items from the vending machine. Once the guard came out to notify them that the two hours were over, they exchanged hugs and kisses good bye. Bryce walked out feeling somewhat relieved that he made his way to visit his mother.

Paris smile was so big and bright, when she saw Bryce walk into the door. As she was chasing Pebbles through the house for chewing up one of her Red Prada Pumps. Paris was so mad at first, but when she saw Bryce walk through the door. She wasn't even thinking about her shoe or the dog.

"Hey, baby!" She ran over to him, giving him a long passionate kiss.

"How was your visit?" She asked. Shocking the hell out of Bryce.

"It was okay. We will talk about that later. How was Brielle's dance recital? I hate that I missed it," Bryce said as he placed his keys on the kitchen counter.

"Oh, Honey! It was great. They won first place," Paris said cheerfully.

"That's what's up! Where is she?" Bryce asked.

"Oh her and the other team mates went out to a burger place, one of the moms are gonna bring her back home."

"Okay, cool!"

Pebbles started barking as a knock came at the door. Paris jumped.

"I'll get it," Bryce said, walking to the door, and Paris fallowed.

Bryce opened the door with a surprised look on his face. There was a guy from the U.S. Postal Service at the door, carrying multiple boxes. There was another, larger box leaning up against the wall on the porch.

"How can I help you?" Bryce asked, as he frowned up when seeing all of the boxes.

"Hello Sir, I need a signature from Bradley Cornell Frost Jr.," he said, gesturing with his clipboard.

Paris immediately cut in, pulling the door wide open. With a confused look on her face.

"Um I'm his mother. What is all of this?"

He laughed nervously. "Oh, Ma'am... I don't know, I'm just delivering it."

"B.J! Come downstairs," Bryce shouted.

"Hey what's going on?" B.J asked, looking worried. Then he noticed all of the boxes.

"Did you order some stuff with that credit card I gave you?" Paris hissed at him.

"No Mom. I only bought two games, and a pair of sneakers, and that was it. I promise.

Paris didn't take her eyes off of B.J, once they got all the boxes inside the house. Bryce went into the garage, and came back with a box cutter. Bryce and B.J Empty out all four boxes. Plus the giant one that was leaning up against the wall, outside on the porch. Paris was damn near foaming at the mouth when she notices the brand new basketball goal that was in the giant box. Then there was the pair of Air Jordan's, Adidas, and Chuck Taylor Sneakers in every color you can imagine. She was livid. Bryce didn't know what to do; he walked in Paris' direction, as she backed away from him. He knew that she was pissed off. B.J still looking at all of the different colored sneakers, and then looking at his mom , still wearing the same pissed off look on her face.

"Dang where did these come from?" B.J asked, still in shock.

"B.J so you mean to tell me that you didn't order all these sneakers, and that damn basketball goal?" Paris was now yelling.

"Mom! No I didn't, half of these sneakers I already have. Well except for this one right here, this playa!" He said picking up the all green Chuck Taylor's.

Paris got even more pissed, and slapped the shoe out of his hand, walking up to him.

"Look! I give you and your brother and sisters everything that you all want, and you go ape shit with the credit card that I gave you. After I told you not to go crazy with it, and you go and do this. You little spoiled ass!" Paris yelled out at him.

"Mom think about it! I already got half of these sneakers in my closet already, so it doesn't make any type of sense for me to go a buy them all over again. Mom you got to believe me I didn't order none of this stuff. B.J pleading with his mom.

"Paris! Look at this! Come here!" Bryce yelled. As he pulled out a light blue card from one of the boxes.

Paris took the card, opened it. Reading the inside with a typed note that read:

"Keep up the heat on the court. You just might go pro someday."

Bryce and Paris locked eyes with each other, after they both read the note inside of the card. They both had an idea of what was going on. Paris dropped the note and the card, when Brielle walked in with a smile. Still wearing her dance costume, carrying two large gift bags. One pink and the other one purple, along with a dozen of red roses.

"Hey Baby, did you have fun?" Paris greeted Brielle as happy as she could, trying to cover up the look of fear and worried that was written all over her face.

"Yes Mom! We had a blast! My dance coach said that someone dropped these beautiful gifts off for me. Gosh, I love being treated like a princess." Brielle giggled, as she skipped over to the couch to open her gifts.

Paris looked over at Bryce, they both rushed into Brielle's direction.

"Honey did your coach tell you who was the person that dropped off these gifts for you?" Bryce asked trying to remain calm.

"Nope!" Brielle smiled.

Paris noticed the white card sticking out of the purple gift bag; she grabs it as Brielle sit on the couch opening her diamond necklace, and yellow canary diamond earrings. Along with a brand new Gucci Backpack. Once Paris got the card open, Bryce ran to her side to, noticing that the card also had a typed note inside. Just like B.J's card.

It read, "You dance like an angel. Keep it up and you'll be a star!"

Paris hands started to shake, and sweat beads appeared on her forehead. She dropped the card, backing away from everyone. Bryce walked over to her.

"Baby calm down, you don't want to scare the kids, I know what you are thinking." Bryce spoke calmly.

"Mom what is wrong?" B.J asked walking over to Paris, but Paris was not able to respond. She was so scared.

"Hey B.J, do me a favor – go pack you and your brother and sisters a bag; we need to go away for a little while. I'll explain everything to you later."

"Okay," B.J responded, going up the stairs to do as he was told.

Paris went into the bedroom to pack some clothes. She continued to shake and sweat, but she was trying to keep calm for her kids. Bryce went into his office, pulled out four bundles of cash from the safe – about twenty-thousand dollars. Then he reached into his desk, grabbing both Silver 380 Caliber Pistols.

He glanced over at the family picture that was sitting on top of his desk and allowed himself to be momentarily lost in his thoughts. He picked up the phone to make a call for conformation that he and Paris weren't tripping, or getting hyped up for nothing. He felt it in his gut that they weren't overreacting; he knew trouble was around the corner, he could feel it.

The operator answered. "Hello, TDC Holiday Unit."

"Um, yes ma'am... I'm planning to come visit my brother tomorrow, I just wanted to make sure that there weren't any visitation restrictions at your facility before I come up there, considering that I will be traveling a very long way." Bryce said.

"Okay Sir. What is your brother's name and TDC Number?" asked the operator.

"His name is Bradley Cornell Frost, and his TDC Number is 1944782." Bryce replied. Then he waited for the Operator to respond, listening to her tap on the computer keys.

"Um Sir, are you sure you gave me the right number?" she said. "I'm not showing an inmate by that name or number in our system."

Bryce gave her the name and number again, and she still wasn't able to find him. Bryce hung up the phone, his nerves jumping all over the place, trying to collect his thoughts, so he could remain calm for his family. But then Paris busted into the office, still a nervous wreck with her hair all over her head.

"Baby, there's a black car parked outside in front of the house." Her voice trembled.

Bryce walks over to her and placed one pistol in her hand. Then he took the other pistol and walked through the door, pulling Paris right along with him.

"Get the kids and go into our bedroom," he ordered.

Paris did as she was told. Bryce peeked out of the side window next to the front door, with his pistol still in hand. He saw the black Monte Carlo outside of the house, the headlights shining brightly onto the street. He watched and waited, then the car sped off, tires screeching. They were definitely going over the speed limit.

Bryce made his way to the bedroom where Paris and all four of the kids were, and was somewhat relieved that Brielle and the twins had fallen asleep. B.J was sitting on the sofa, holding Paris in his arms. Bryce knew that he really didn't have to worry too much about B.J – he was intelligent for his age, and he had a damn good understanding. Bryce looked over at the kids, still sound asleep, then noticed multiple duffle bags packed up in the corner against the wall.

He clapped his hands. "Okay, let's get out of here," he said, motioning for Paris to help him grab the bags. "We're taking the Tahoe. Paris, call your dad and sister and let them know what's going on. Have them pack a bag and hit Interstate 10." Five minutes later, everyone was loaded into the Tahoe and Paris was buckling herself up. Bryce handed her an Atlas Map Book. "Here, pick a place."

Then they were winding their way out of the neighborhood and toward the highway. Paris sighed deeply, allowing herself to relax into her seat for a few minutes. Then she looked at the city through the rear view mirror. It was time to kiss Houston goodbye.

www.ingramcontent.com/pod-product-compliance
Lightning Source LLC
Chambersburg PA
CBHW071946040426
42447CB00024B/1451